Blessing Your Grown Children

BLESSING *Your* GROWN CHILDREN

Debra Evans

Tyndale House Publishers, Inc.
Carol Stream, Illinois

Also by Debra Evans

A Focus on the Family book published by
Tyndale House Publishers, Inc., Carol Stream, Illinois 60188

Focus on the Family and the accompanying logo and design are federally registered trademarks of Focus on the Family, Colorado Springs, CO 80995.

TYNDALE and Tyndale's quill logo are registered trademarks of Tyndale House Publishers, Inc.

Editor: Brandy Bruce
Designed by Jacqueline L. Nuñez
Cover photograph of family in field copyright © Westend61/Corbis. All rights reserved.
Cover photograph of adults copyright © Eric Audras/PhotoAlto/Corbis. All rights reserved.
Cover photograph copyright © Image Source Photography <http://marketplace.veer.com>/stock-photo/-ISP0047006 /Veer. All rights reserved.

Library of Congress Cataloging-in-Publication Data
Evans, Debra.
  Blessing your grown children / by Debra Evans.
    p. cm.
  Includes bibliographical references (p.   ) and index.
  ISBN 978-1-4143-6460-5 (alk. paper)
  1. Parenting——Religious aspects——Christianity. 2. Parent and adult child——Religious aspects——Christianity. I. Title.
  BV4529.E88 2012
  248.8′45—dc23
                          2011041218

ISBN: 978-1-58997-479-1

Printed in the United States of America
1 2 3 4 5 6 7 8 9 /17 16 15 14 13 12

To my dad and mom, John and Nancy Munger,
whose love and blessing encourage me still.
To my husband and partner in parenting, David,
with whom I continue to share each step along the way
by the grace of our generous Father.

CONTENTS

A NOTE ABOUT THE
PEOPLE IN THIS BOOK

For the sake of protecting everyone's privacy, with the exception of my family's privacy in certain instances, I have changed the names of the people whose stories I shared in this book, and in various cases I have created composites of their stories based on the conversations and correspondence I have had the privilege of sharing with them. In every case, I obtained permission from the people I wrote about before including them in *Blessing Your Grown Children*. I trust you will gain encouragement and understanding as you consider the familiar themes, questions, and concerns voiced by so many of my valued friends, colleagues, and acquaintances.

INTRODUCTION

When we ask God to bless our families, how do we partner with Him in this endeavor? What means are available to us in this pursuit?

These are the two main questions I invite you to explore with me as you read *Blessing Your Grown Children*.

When I began working on this book, my husband, Dave, and I were living alone at our house in Austin, Texas, our adopted hometown for the past eighteen years. Our adult children, having long since left home, were then residing in a variety of places in Texas and Colorado, with only one of them choosing to settle nearby.

Given our fairly predictable "now that the kids are grown" daily routine at the time, I had every reason to expect that the writing process would be a relatively straightforward experience involving about fifteen weeks' worth of extended retreats spent in the quiet calm of my household office.

But before we knew it, all three of our long-gone grown kids unexpectedly returned to live in Austin, with two of them temporarily moving back into our home.

The first thing to go was my office. I quickly packed, pushed, and piled everything from the two bedrooms where our son and daughter would be staying into the spare, windowless space I've always used for writing. That was the easy part. After all, laptops are ideally designed for off-site use and easy portability, aren't they?

The second thing that went was my writing schedule. As our children one by one faced large life transitions and complex crises—emergency-room visits and hospitalizations, new jobs, a third pregnancy following two miscarriages within the same year, heart surgery, long-distance relocations, financial stresses, challenges related to coping with chronic illness, and more—my husband and I rearranged our daily plans as needed. We also found ourselves coming face-to-face with our past, present, and future roles as parents.

The third thing to disappear was my rough draft of this book. When I realized the manuscript I had been working on didn't offer the most important ideas and suggestions that *I* needed to think about, consider, and learn from as a suddenly-and-truly-we're-now-deep-in-the-thick-of-things second-stage parent, I started over. Looking back, I think there was much more God wanted to teach me, by experience, before I shared with you what seems to work best and what doesn't when it comes to blessing our adult children.

I offer my suggestions now not because I've become an expert on this subject, but because I believe that no matter what comes up on our parenting journey, God is there and His wisdom and help are constantly available to us when we seek Him. Page by page, I want to pass this encouragement along to you.

If you picked up *Blessing Your Grown Children* thinking that it's possible to bless your adult son or daughter while remaining at a safe distance from his or her struggles and your imperfections, you may not want to continue reading past this sentence. On the other hand, if you, like me, find yourself traveling through an unpredictable and sometimes tumultuous landscape in which God appears to be inviting us to trust Him in new ways, please keep reading.

Before Going Further:
Is This Book for Me?

Please check any of the following statements that currently apply to your relationship with your adult child:

❑ I desire to invest the gifts of my time, material resources, wisdom, and love in my adult child's life, but it's sometimes challenging to find the right balance.

❑ I want to bless my grown child, but I'm not sure how to go about it.

❑ I'd like to enlarge my appreciation for the meaning of "blessing" as an action of word, deed, or intentional prayer for the benefit of my adult child and to learn how to practice it more wisely.

❑ As a parent, I hope to avoid the problems that may arise from my doing too little or too much, not letting go, holding on to the past, and not learning from my earlier mistakes.

❑ I want to grow in my understanding of how to compassionately and considerately express my love for my grown child.

❑ I occasionally, or often, feel uncertain about my role and responsibilities as the parent of an adult child.

❑ I want to more consistently acknowledge and not be afraid to admit to my adult child my mistakes, limitations, and imperfections when it's appropriate to do so.

❑ I want to more intentionally practice blessing my grown child as an expression of the love God has given me for my family and as a reflection of my relationship with Christ.

❑ I feel pressured by or uncomfortable around others when they talk about their adult child's accomplishments because my son or daughter is experiencing physical, emotional, vocational, relational, and/or spiritual difficulty right now.

❑ I like/don't like the person my grown child seems to be becoming, and I want to focus on entrusting God's good plans and purposes for his or her life.

❑ I see some similar personality traits and lifestyle habits in my adult son or daughter that I see in myself, bringing both challenges and opportunities to our maturing relationship.

❑ Sometimes I'm unclear about my role in helping my adult child leave the nest.

❑ I'd like to stop measuring my success as a parent based on what my adult child does and doesn't do.

❑ I'm open to taking the next steps in my parenting journey with an emphasis on loving, valuing, cherishing, and accepting my grown child as an independent adult.

If you checked one or more of the boxes in this list, welcome to *Blessing Your Grown Children*. Whatever is happening today in our lives, wherever we live, it is my hope that these pages will be a reminder of the vital part we have yet to play in blessing our children in the midst of life as it actually is right now. Glad to be here with you.

PART I

The Questions: Learning as We Go

*The Lord is gracious and full of
compassion, slow to anger and great in
mercy. The Lord is good to all, and His
tender mercies are over all His works.*

—Psalm 145:8-9, NKJV

*This is what all the work of grace
aims at—an ever-deeper knowledge of
God, and an ever-closer relationship
with Him.*

—J. I. Packer

CHAPTER ONE

What's Next?

*To perceive and then to decide—God
does not show us the whole way but
only the next step.*
—Ingrid Trobisch

"The heart has its reasons, of which reason knows nothing," the French philosopher Blaise Pascal once wisely observed.

These classic words carry the ring of truth. Today, as I watched our oldest daughter backing her car out of our driveway, for an instant the grown woman she has become seemed to suddenly vanish, leaving in her wake the unforgotten image of a giggling towheaded toddler climbing into her molded plastic car seat.

Joanna is now a creative and motivated mother of two amazing daughters not unlike herself. Her day-to-day schedule keeps her going from the moment she gets out of bed in the morning, providing little rest until her head sinks back down into the pillow at night.

No question about it—every day my daughter energetically confronts the rewards and risks associated with her adult independence, no parental supervision required. Even so, every once in a while, whenever I unexpectedly catch a glimpse of Joanna's budding former self in my mind's eye, tears have a way of springing up as I watch her once again step out our door.

This morning, a photo of Joanna's baby dedication caught my

Stephanie and Patrick

I've known Stephanie since we were teenagers. No longer located in the same state, we stay in touch by phone, praying for and with each other regularly. Through the years of being young brides, first-time mothers, and parents of school-age children, not once did she and I imagine that we would someday be faced with the challenges associated with grown children affected by life-threatening chronic health conditions.

A few years year ago, Stephanie called, her voice shaking. She told me her son, Patrick, was missing after abandoning his car hours earlier in downtown Detroit. It was unclear whether he was still alive. After she explained to me the details she knew so far, we immediately began praying.

As we did, one of Patrick's friends called on Stephanie's cell phone; I could hear him saying that he had located Patrick, who appeared to be experiencing a manic episode related to the bipolar disorder he lives with. He was threatening to harm himself. The police were there and an ambulance had arrived. It was likely that Patrick would be transported to a state behavioral-care hospital and admitted for treatment.

"I don't know if I can handle this, Debra," Stephanie told me later that night.

"I know how you feel," I replied.

We both sat in silence, too sad to cry.

attention. Looking closely at the familiar image of our daughter snuggled in my arms, I thought, *The longer I travel this parenting journey, the more it feels as if the road I'm on has taken me in a much different direction than I expected.*

"This isn't what I pictured it would be like," she said.

"Me either, Steph."

"What am I going to do? How can I help Patrick? Tell me this is going to get better. Tell me this won't ever happen again. Tell me what to do with this terrible pain I feel ripping across the center of my chest."

"I know what you mean," I whispered.

"I know you do."

"So, we're not giving up. No matter what it looks like or how it feels right now," I acknowledged, "you and I have seen what God alone has done and what only He can do."

"We have." On the other end of the phone, I heard Stephanie take a deep breath, hold it, and then exhale slowly.

We both sat in silence for several minutes, turning our thoughts toward the one sure source of help we knew.

"Steph, the cross is bigger than this."

"Yes, it is, Debra."

Long silence. Space to breathe. Time to remember.

"God is with us. Jesus left the ninety-nine to go after the one wandering alone in the wild. A little while ago, Stephanie, Patrick was nowhere to be found."

"Let's keep praying."

It doesn't matter how old they are. Regardless of my adult children's independence and abilities, I still find myself wanting to shelter them from the storms that can arise without warning, from the pain and brokenness of our fallen world, and thereby somehow guide them away from unseen danger back to safety.

Yes, I know. Of course this isn't reasonable. I believe God can and does do this and much, much more—perfectly—all the time.

I acknowledge and accept my limits. I really do.

So, when it comes to the adult-to-adult relationship I share with my now-grown children, how can I fully explain my heart's steady resistance to my head's studied logic?

Where is your heart resisting your head's logic today? Perhaps you're trying to adjust to your empty nest, or you might be dealing with an adult child who has made a few costly choices that have presented you with some hard decisions about the boundaries you need to set.

Like my friend Theresa, whose thirty-two-year-old developmentally disabled daughter lives at home, you may find your chronic sorrow getting in the way of your ability to think clearly about what is needed. For Daniel, his biggest challenge as a father lies in knowing how much and when to intervene when his son with substance-abuse disorder relapses. Or maybe you can relate to Kate and Stephen, who sometimes lie awake at night wondering what happened with their grown daughters, neither of whom considers herself a Christian.

Are we ready to move beyond our resistance to accepting our sons and daughters not for who we want them to be but as the men and women they actually are? As we go through this book together, we'll take a closer look at our longing for control in situations like these and how we can recognize and surrender this desire. I'll ask you to examine and expand your ideas about what it means to find happiness and success as a parent. I will also encourage you to draw near to and depend on God more deeply as you extend the blessings you receive from Him to your adult child.

From Intimacy to Independence

While our relationships with our spouses and best friends began with distant nonacquaintance and gradually moved toward more familiar ways of sharing, our parenthood began not with a wave of hello but with our baby's conception—the most intimate human connection imaginable.

From the earliest moments, the magnitude of the gift was made real: This child is God's masterpiece, created in His image, designed for His purpose, brought to life for His glory . . .

We accepted responsibility for this gift, believing that our child would forever belong to his or her Creator, not to us. We understood that our son or daughter would be with us only for a limited time. We accepted our unwritten job description, acknowledged the daily investment required, and appreciated the enduring nature of our role. But somewhere in the midst of walking through the next twenty years, it was often easy to forget our destination. Though we realized from the start that the goal of our attachment was our child's detachment from us, the temporary focus of our occupation felt as if it was permanent.

Before parenthood, we didn't understand the depth of the sacrifice, the scope of the demands, the cost of the commitment. As the baby's due date approached, we made room and stocked the nursery while wondering what having another person living in the house would be like. Our options narrowed concerning how we would spend our time, our money, and our Saturday mornings. Slowly but surely we climbed the mountain and faced our fears on the way up. Remember?

Upon happily receiving our child into our arms at the grand finale of those nine months of intimate nurture, we found we had not only given birth to our first child, but we had also been given birth into a new identity ourselves.

Mother . . . Father. The words sounded as if they belonged to someone else, reminding us of our parents. Day by day and night by night, we responded to the call of our valuable vocation. Years passed. We gradually recognized the true meaning of our title.

Every day, whether we actively thought about it or not, we drew nearer to distancing ourselves from this most important job. More questions presented themselves; some remain unanswered: Will he stay safe and healthy? How will she use her God-given gifts and talents? When will he come to know Christ? Whom will she marry, if anyone? Where will he live? Is her income enough to meet her expenses? What if he makes the wrong choices? In which direction will she go if she fails?

Now that we're here, on this other side of the parenting journey, it's clear that the time has come, in a sense, to give birth once again. It is in this stage of parenting, where no ceremonies, showers, or celebrations commemorate our new role, that our children are birthed into their independence.

An Unpredictable Path

My friend Pam tells me that when her two sons were young, she often imagined what her life might be like when, at long last, they were finally grown up and living on their own:

No more settling ugly sibling-rivalry disputes! No more car-pools! An end, at last, to irritating animal noises, extensive pediatrician's visits, huge laundry pileups, interrupted sleep, safety-locked cabinets, and regularly recurring messes!

There were days when it seemed as if life would never be "normal" again, when the thought of the kids launching out on their own seemed so far off in the distance, I began doubt-ing it would ever actually happen. I pictured my husband and myself going on long cruises together, blissfully sailing toward some faraway exotic harbor.

I thought about what it would be like to be able to get out my watercolor box and sit outdoors painting for hours on end without anyone shouting, "Mom! Hurry! Come quickly! I need you!" I could sign up for a cooking class and make an entire meal consisting of the foods only Chris and I would enjoy eating. Needless to say, we'd also sleep long hours on weekends together, without locking our bedroom door.

Now that her sons are thirty and thirty-two, with the eldest liv-ing at the family's home following grad school and business setbacks, Pam realizes that the joys and challenges of parenting her boys dur-ing their early years were relatively simple and straightforward tasks compared to coping with the post-childhood, second-stage parent-ing complexities she now faces.

While my friend has done many of the fun and fabulous things she once imagined doing—taking a Caribbean cruise, painting nature scenes outdoors, making Greek stew with marinated lamb and cous-cous salad, sleeping in late on Saturdays—not once did she picture herself indefinitely residing under the same roof with her grown child.

Rather than dwell in the past, move into your new home—second-stage parenting. See what's next. Accept your offspring's adulthood. Actively support your son's or daughter's autonomy. Stay focused on the big picture.

Can you relate to Pam's situation? The truth is that making the transition from parenting young kids to understanding, accepting, and loving our grown children, adult to adult, is an unpredictable process for which there is no foolproof recipe.

Present Grace

We bring the entire history of our parenting experiences into every encounter we share with our adult children, and while delightful memories of distant events remain alive in our hearts—inevitably provoking a smile, or tears, at random moments—there is no turning back to an earlier time. There is only moving forward, no matter what today looks like.

Even if we can't go back, we can face this moment and bring something good to it. Through prayerfully and mindfully letting go, moving beyond the past, and acknowledging what lies behind us, we can turn toward the future with God's present grace.

When our kids were young, our parenting efforts concentrated on promoting their well-being, shaping their character, and guiding their decision making. Now that we're no longer responsible for them in any of these areas, what's next? How do we let go of our most consuming concerns for our grown children and change our focus? Are we ready to accept them as they are and surrender to God our preoccupation with our expectations of them? When will we trust Him more fully with our maturing family's care?

Learning how to lovingly affirm and wisely support our grown kids as we let them go—letting them know they are accepted and valued based on who they are rather than on what they achieve or believe—requires humility, a genuine desire for God's leading, and a willingness to change. A quote widely attributed to Corrie ten Boom advises us: "Hold everything in your hands lightly—otherwise it hurts when God pries your fingers open."

Like learning how to nurture our children when they were younger, blessing them as adults is a series of choices we make rather than a process we instantly or easily acquire. Rather than constantly picturing our grown kids turning out a certain way, we decide again and again that we will love and cherish them not because of what they do, but for who they are.

What strengthens our parent-child bond post-childhood? Which healthy strategies will we choose to apply as a means of nurturing and maintaining our adult parent–adult child relationships? When

Decide that you won't correct or try to redirect, subtly or not so subtly, your adult child's behavior for something specific he or she has recently said or done. Seek God's wisdom, forgive your son or daughter, set boundaries if needed, and keep moving forward.

the going gets tough or we miss being with our grown children, how shall we bless them while valuing and respecting their adult independence?

By better understanding the limits of our God-given responsibility and acquiring wisdom regarding the ways to bless our grown children, we'll strengthen and refresh our relationship with them, nurturing it by our actions, attitudes, and prayers in the midst of human frailty and imperfection. In seeking God and His wisdom first, we find we're able to discern and embrace more fully the vital role we have yet to play.

Words to Remember

- Wise men and women are always learning, always listening for fresh insights. (Proverbs 18:15, MSG)
- There is a time for everything, and a season for every activity under heaven. (Ecclesiastes 3:1)
- I know that you can do all things; no purpose of yours can be thwarted. (Job 42:2)

Real Adults Share Their Stories

For a long time, my mom just didn't seem to get me at all. We're very different, and as I've grown older, it felt like we had less rather than more in common. The distance between us eventually grew to the point where I didn't want to call or visit her.

When Mom called and encouraged me to spend a week with her and Dad at their summer home, something in her voice let me know that she was more willing to listen to what I had to say.

I'm glad she reached out and left the decision up to me. Her willingness to stop being defensive about the past and put her focus on the present—the positive strengths and experiences we're now building upon—has been encouraging. We've laughed and cried together in ways I didn't experience with her when I was younger.

I'm not sure how or why this happened, but if I had to guess, I'd say Mom finally missed me enough to come to terms with the fact that I'm not the person she thinks I should be. While her acceptance doesn't mean we don't disagree—we still do, of course—it does mean I find her easier to talk to and be around. And that's been an amazing gift for us both.

—Natalie

For Personal Reflection

1. Before my child became an adult, I used to think . . .
2. Once my child was an adult, I realized . . .
3. As I look toward the future, my role as a parent seems to be . . .

Prayers

Praying God's Blessing for My Family
O my soul, bless God. From head to toe, I'll bless His holy name! O my soul, bless God, don't forget a single blessing! He forgives our sins—every one. He heals our diseases—every one. He redeems us from hell—saves our lives! He crowns us with love and mercy—a paradise crown. He wraps us in goodness—beauty eternal. He renews our youth—we're always young in His presence. God makes everything come out right; He puts victims back on their feet. (Adaptation of Psalm 103:1-6, MSG)

Praying God's Blessing for My Grown Child
I ask—ask the God of our Master, Jesus Christ, the God of glory—
to make you intelligent and discerning in knowing him personally,
your eyes focused and clear, so that you can see exactly what it is he
is calling you to do, grasp the immensity of this glorious way of life
he has for his followers, oh, the utter extravagance of his work in
us who trust him—endless energy, boundless strength! (Ephesians
1:17-19, MSG)

Blessings Now

- Take a closer look at your expectations of your grown child
  at present. Write down as many as you can think of; then
  identify the three or four on your list that seem the most
  unrealistic. Extend grace instead of criticism in the coming
  years to your son or daughter in these areas.
- Look at your son or daughter in person or in a recent photograph. If your son or daughter is or isn't actively following Christ at present, in what ways does this affect the way
  you see him or her? How will you seek to find God's image
  reflected in your imperfect adult child (as well as yourself)
  today?
- Consider what it means to you to help your grown child.
  If you're offering your support as a way to feel better about
  yourself, experience less loneliness, alleviate his or her
  responsibility, ease your guilt, look good to others, and/or
  exercise parental control, you could be hurting more than
  helping. Ask yourself how your help may be adding to
  or detracting from your son's or daughter's adult need to

(1) find ways to set and achieve goals, (2) accept responsibility for decisions, (3) enjoy accomplishments, and (4) learn from mistakes.

- Before offering your help, think it through as much as possible, keeping your adult child's best interests in mind and setting necessary limits where needed. Remember that if something is important enough to your adult child, he or she will be willing to think, act, and work to make it happen.

- Understand your limitations and use your influence wisely. Don't treat your grown-up child like a little kid. Instead, take your relationship to the next level. Recognize and affirm by your words and actions that you value your adult-to-adult relationship. View your grown son or daughter as capable of leading his or her own life.

- Review your definition of parental "success" and determine where it came from. If it involves comparing yourself and your grown child to others, you may be experiencing feelings of frustration, inadequacy, and disappointment. For the rest of the week, pay attention to your ongoing thoughts in this regard. Confront any "if only" or "what might have been" detours as they arise in your mind with the reality of God's loving, life-giving grace.

- Keep being a positive role model for your adult child. Love faithfully; live generously; remain confident that your actions will always speak louder than your words. Your son or daughter is still influenced by your attitudes, values, behavior, and beliefs, which may yet encourage him or her to make meaningful changes.

Getting and Staying Unstuck

Where do you most want God to bring change, renewal, and restoration to your relationship with your grown child? Put simply, we're no longer in charge of our grown children's choices or responsible for the choices they make. In exchange for the unnecessary burdens we take on by wanting to control the uncontrollable and trying to fix the unfixable, with God's help and the wise support of others we can see where changes are needed now. If and when we get stuck in this area, we can set specific boundaries with our adult children and start moving in a new direction.

Getting Unstuck
Consider the following questions and answer them honestly.

1. What changes are needed most in my relationship with my adult child?

2. Am I willing to make these necessary changes?

3. How do I view the changes I need to make?

4. What will be gained and what will be lost if I make these changes?

5. Where do I need to place boundaries to provide for and protect the changes I need to make?

6. Who are the safe people with whom I will remain open and accountable about my decisions concerning these necessary changes?

Staying Unstuck

Surround yourself with safe people who believe you can change, who encourage your efforts to make needed changes, and with whom you can pray about these changes:

- *Gain new perspective and encouragement from professionals trained to work with adults in transition,* including marriage and family counselors, pastors, licensed psychologists, therapists, social workers, spiritual directors, addiction experts, educators, and health-care providers. Determining which professionals are best suited to help you will depend on what you need, what their approach is, who is available, and where you are located, as well as how much time and money you can afford to spend. If you need a referral, ask someone acquainted with family resources in your area whose opinion you value, or call Focus on the Family (800-A-Family).

- *Let the people in your support network know that you want to make changes in your relationship with your grown child.* Tell them about how, when, and where you want to make changes. Ask them to hold you accountable for your decisions by posing relevant questions, prompting you in the desired direction, and offering constructive suggestions.

- *Pray with select members of your team on a regular basis.* Refuse to stay stuck by becoming spiritually isolated. Seek God's life-changing wisdom, help, and direction with your spouse and others, recalling Christ's promise: "When two of you get together on anything at all on earth and make a prayer of it, my Father in heaven goes into action. And when two or three of you are together because of me, you can be sure that I'll be there" (Matthew 18:19-20, MSG).

CHAPTER TWO

Where's My Focus?

To escape the distress caused by regret
for the past or fear about the future,
this is the rule to follow: Leave the past
to the infinite mercy of God, the future
to His good providence; give the present
wholly to His love by being faithful to
His grace.

—Jean-Pierre de Caussade

Debra,

Thanks for chatting yesterday. For a very long time, I have said that the toughest thing to watch or experience is a parent losing a child. Although I believe that is the hardest thing I have watched and experienced in my family, I know that there are circumstances that are as painful . . . and more challenging in many ways.

I have seen it and still see it with Dan's family and my brother-in-law who struggles with substance abuse. I have felt it when our daughter Andrea takes issue with me, explains to her dad that I just don't understand her (and she doesn't want to talk with me), or rationalizes her position by generalizing—saying that she doesn't fit in with our family. Those blaming, irrational reactions and generalizations are my clue that "something else" is happening. I may never know what it is, and I certainly can't fix it, but her words and actions are hurtful.

Our adult children are making adult choices, some more painful to watch than others. Like you, I pray for wisdom and the divine intervention of our dear Papa, who loves Andi more unconditionally than I do.

With love,

Mary

Parenthood is permanent—a lifelong identity, an ongoing sacred trust, the bond that will not quit. Our enduring family connections are cemented together by much more than shared DNA. Based upon God-given intimacy and interdependence, gradually forged in the fiery places of love and sacrifice, the deep attachment we share with our children doesn't appear to be designed to blossom into the kind of once-and-for-all detachment other species experience, does it?

Year after year we keep carrying our grown children close to our hearts, caring deeply about their well-being. As we do, our minds don't always accept the limitations imposed by childhood's end. We may try doing more rather than less when our grown kids' real experiences don't follow our ideal plans for them. We may lean toward attempting to assert our parental authority rather than letting go of our children and respecting their need for independence from us.

Our shifting parental position, at times, can cause us to cling to the Lord as never before. Wisdom leads us to understand our current limitations and our influence. Instead of seeking to seize control, we can recognize signs of God's help and handiwork in all stages of life.

Handing Over the Keys

Recently, my husband, Dave, recounted one of his favorite memories of staying at our family's cabin twenty-five years ago. His summer vacation story became a thoughtful prelude to a three-hour conversation discussing our perspectives on lifelong parenting:

> I can still see the six of us coming in from the boat, with all of you running toward the cabin and me putting the hot dogs on the grill. A pile of beach towels sat nearby in the sand. The smell of the suntan lotion filled the air as the kids ran past me again and start splashing in the water.
>
> None of us seemed like we had a care in the world. Being together having fun at the lake was so good. . . .
>
> Most evenings, after I came in from fishing, we would either spend the rest of the night sitting around the campfire roasting marshmallows or staying inside the cabin, where we played games and watched movies. Sometimes we would head back outside late in the evening, walking barefoot through the wet grass to the dock, carrying our flashlights and blankets.
>
> We often enjoyed looking at the stars together—remember the way the kids acted? They couldn't quite believe their eyes. Often the night sky appeared as if God had splashed a can of white paint across the heavens. Once or twice we spotted the Northern Lights shimmering high above us.
>
> There was a sense of ease to those summer days like nothing else. When I think of those days we spent together, it

seemed like they'd last forever. It's still hard for me to believe how quickly time has gone by.

Hearing my husband talk about being with our kids at our family's cabin up north proved a poignant contrast to what he said next. When I asked him to describe a specific turning point in our children's up-and-coming independence, without hesitation Dave declared, "That's easy! The day they got their driver's licenses." Then he added,

> For years I felt a certain sense of control as a parent based on the role God had given me. Childrearing, though demanding, was a privilege—as satisfying and rewarding a personal involvement as I've ever had.
>
> The big moment came when it was time for each child to take off alone behind the wheel. After I had spent years talking to our kids about cars, speed limits, driving defensively, and the rules of the road, the moment inevitably arrived when I stepped out of the driver's seat, handed over the keys, and waved good-bye. I felt both proud and queasy.
>
> Despite the fact that I knew I wouldn't always be responsible for making choices for our children, over the years I'd become used to exercising my authority as their dad. More than anything, this one area highlighted my changing role within our family. No matter how well the kids had been prepared for this next step or how much we had prayed for them, their driving independence represented risks beyond my fatherly control.

As Dave spoke, I instantly recalled what it felt like to hand over the keys. Like him, I remember thinking, *Okay, steady now. Take a deep breath. The future has arrived.* Impressive as that milestone was, the moment itself was exceptionally sobering.

Because we knew the risks as well as the benefits represented by

The First Father

I remember a sunny summer day in Paris when I knelt in a beautiful park to pray for a second child. Four years had passed since the birth of our first child, and we were impatient for a larger family. As time passed we consulted clinics, but our apparent infertility had no physiological explanation. My prayer was earnest but routine. It included an oft-repeated clause in my proposed contract with God, which ran roughly, "Of course I want the child to be a credit both to me and to you. I would like him or her to be a true disciple of Jesus Christ. Otherwise, I would rather do without."

A thought exploded like a bomb in my brain. From the cloudless blue the reply seemed to come, "What about me and Adam?"

Instantly I knew what he was saying. God had not made us automata but had created us in his image with wills of our own and therefore with the capacity to choose to please God or to displease him, to obey him or to rebel against him. We chose not God's way but our own. . . .

Was I willing, like God, to give the gift of life whatever the consequences might be, no matter how my child might choose to use that life? A hundred ugly possibilities flashed on the screen of my mind. A growing fear filled me. I was asking God to let me bring life into being. He was telling me I would not have control of what the fruit of my body might do with the life I gave. Was I still willing to give life to someone who might bring me humiliation, pain, disgrace?

—Dr. John White[1]

our children driving and entering adulthood, our celebration came with a sigh. Though we knew all along that our previous parenting patterns must shift to accommodate the new attitudes and behaviors that increasingly recognized and respected our children's adulthood, the big task of stepping back as they moved forward looked very different to us once the future arrived.

Whatever the Consequences

Let's be honest. We didn't completely count the cost on the front end.

Even if once upon a time we had considered the overwhelming question—whether we were willing, "like God, to give the gift of life whatever the consequences might be, no matter how [our] child might choose to use that life"—how far did we actually get in measuring the distance we would eventually travel?

As Dave reminded me during our talk that evening:

While at times I find myself recalling when the kids were younger and I could more easily guide them, often I'm impressed by and proud of their ability to navigate the world. Many of our daughters' and sons' choices have been excep-. tional, better than ours in similar circumstances. Some of their choices have been really difficult to come to terms with. I really wish I could have spared them the pain of those decisions.

It helps me to keep remembering: Our grown children's choices are their birthright and their responsibility—choices about what they believe about God, where and how they live and work and think and relax and spend their money, who their friends are, whether they attend church or not (not to mention the type of church they attend), whom and when they marry, whether or not they have children, and much more. Not one of these decisions is ours to make.

Remember God and Adam.

These last four words stopped me in my tracks.

Given that God—the only perfect Parent who always, unfailingly, 100 percent of the time gets it right—formed as His first child the man who got it so wrong, what does this mean for us . . . and our children . . . and their children?

I suspect it means that no matter what, at minimum you and I are going to have some unmet expectations.

Most parents I know carry in their hearts an unwritten list of dreams and desires concerning their children. Many of us have seen our children fulfill or exceed our expectations. And many of us have not.

Though we may sometimes long for a way to return to an earlier, simpler time when we could shelter our sons and daughters and easily mend many of their problems, today God is giving us a clear opportunity: From this day forward, we can love them with open arms, adult to adult, while learning to trust our Father ever more deeply with our grown children's care, help, guidance, and protection, as well as our own.

When your grown child makes a decision you don't fully understand, agree with, or approve of, how do you respond? What do you do and say when he or she makes choices that differ from what you think is best?

A wider vista has opened up before us, whole unexplored regions where God's persistent grace and the frailties of human faith are distinctly within view. Here, God's grace appears even brighter, His mercy and unfailing love even more astonishing.

Remember God and Adam.

Christine and Megan

It took several years for Christine to gain the required knowledge and necessary experience for her employment as a corporate wellness consultant. As a competitive gymnast, she had earlier developed a personal appreciation for energy-enhancing fitness that she still enjoys sharing with others. Her daughter Megan, a quiet culinary-arts-school graduate and pastry chef at a downtown restaurant in Denver, couldn't care less.

Christine, who weighs sixty-eight pounds less than her same-height daughter, spent more than a dozen years trying to motivate Megan to eat healthier and reduce her size—hinting, urging, criticizing, and arguing about food; bringing up all kinds of weight-loss goals and strategies; discussing various exercise classes and programs—by talking about everything sideways, as if it was only about her own struggle to stay fit. She describes it as being "like I was blind and deaf, completely unable to see or hear the messages Megan was receiving," until she took a class and read a book about eating disorders.

Since starting to acknowledge the impact of her attitudes, Christine has sought expert help for herself. She now recognizes the importance of boundaries and is working on more fully accepting and appreciating herself, and her daughter, in view of God's unchanging love.

No Longer Our Responsibility

As the mother of four adult children—now all in their thirties, with the days of our spending time together at the family's cabin long behind us—I find each day that I need to depend on God more, pray more, and learn more concerning my grown kids. And not all days are created equal regarding the level of abiding care and concern I feel, even with God's constantly available care and help.

As the challenges and concerns come up, Dave and I don't automatically know how to respond—what to say, where to find the necessary support, whom to seek advice from, and how much of our time, money, and energy to give.

Take today, for example. Dave called me from his car on his way to work, as he usually does most weekday mornings, so we could continue talking and praying about the things currently at the top of our list, including

- Jon's and Ali's current housing questions and their plans to relocate because of recent crime in their neighborhood;
- Katy's bite from a brown recluse spider, as well as her new job, where she won't be receiving health-care coverage;
- David's (hopefully temporary) layoff from work and his immediate need for employment support and supplemental income; and
- Joanna's responsibility for chairing an upcoming fund-raising event.

In asking God for His wisdom, help, and blessing concerning these things and many more, we believe the part we still have to play is vitally important. Though our grown children's choices and the consequences that follow are not our responsibility, our prayers, our responses, and our love will always matter.

*Are you open to reaching out to and receiving support
from others with whom you can share this parenting journey? As your grown children continue their
course toward greater maturity, seek wise advice.
Obtain ample prayer support. Invite others to join
you in affirming your grown children's adult status.
Look toward God for what only He can do.*

How We Grow

Though we cannot survey the entire picture yet, we can rest in the
assurance that the Lord unfailingly loves our children and us as He
faithfully works everything together for their good and ours, even in
the details of the most difficult circumstances.

Yes, I know. It's much easier to see this when things are going
well.

For my friends Diane and Steven, their son Josh's four-year de-
tention in a state correctional facility for a DUI presented them with
questions they had never considered, let alone expected to face.

"What does it mean to bless your grown child while he's incarcerated at one of the nation's toughest prisons as the result of a
series of illegal alcohol-related decisions, with no clear release date in
sight?" Diane asked me.

"The last time I heard from Josh, he wrote that he was being
housed in a cage with fifty-seven men with open toilet and shower
facilities in the center. Every time I picture Josh being there, locked
up in a metal enclosure without any personal privacy, surrounded
by all those potentially violent guys, the only way I can stop myself
from sinking into despair is to cry out to God, asking Him to pro-

tect and help my son, and pray as long and as often as I need to.

"Knowing I can't change Josh's circumstances is the most difficult thing we've yet faced," Diane said honestly.

Instead of seeking to conquer or control, like Diane and Steven we can reach for and recognize God's help. Opening our eyes to His truth and receiving His grace with gratitude, we gain glimpses of fresh hope.

It is here, at these times, often in the most confusing places, that we can most vividly see ourselves and our adult children as we actually are—our perfect God's own imperfect, beloved sons and daughters, blessed with our Father's great love, redemption, and grace.

When we apply this new lens through which we can examine our roles in second-stage parenting, we're increasingly able to view our relationships with our grown children as the most important value. *The relationships we share*—not our parenting successes and failures nor our met and unmet expectations for our children—*become an expression of our highest calling*. By placing our focus on Christ where it belongs, we come closer to partnering with God in loving our adult children.

Are you willing to believe God will do what you cannot do for yourself and your family? Can you see that in your imperfections and weaknesses, God will never stop loving you and your grown children?

Fear and anxiety about the past, present, and future of your parent-child bond can drain life from your relationship. Consider and apply these constructive responses as an alternative:

- Understand that perfect parenting is impossible.
- Accept God's forgiveness for your mistakes.
- Give yourself credit for the things you've done and are doing well.
- Keep learning.

Words to Remember

- We do not know what to do, but our eyes are on you.
  (2 Chronicles 20:12, ESV)
- Cast all your anxiety on him because he cares for you.
  (1 Peter 5:7)
- Steep your life in God-reality, God-initiative, God-provisions. Don't worry about missing out. You'll find all your everyday human concerns will be met. (Matthew 6:33, MSG)

Real Adults Share Their Stories

I'm almost thirty now. I love my mom and dad, but I don't want to hear their advice unless I ask them for it. I don't appreciate it when they keep telling me what they think I should do, or when they won't back off on the phone calls when I need some space.

It feels like both my parents still see me as a kid. If they would just listen to me when I try to talk with them, it would help a lot. I'm not sure they know how.

Here's what I would say to my parents if they asked for my honest opinion about a way they could really bless me:

See me as an adult. See the good and amazing parts of me as well as those things that aren't as great, the things that frustrate or irritate you, or the things you don't agree with.

Focus on what's positive, my strengths instead of my weaknesses. Don't forget I'm doing my best.

And *please listen*.

I'll try to do all of the same things for you.

—Lee

For Personal Reflection

1. Trusting God will do what I cannot do when it comes to my adult child means I must . . .
2. In times of conflict with my adult child, I find hope in seeing . . .
3. Valuing my relationship with my adult child encourages me to focus on . . .

Prayers

Praying God's Blessing for My Family

Clean the slate, God, so we can start the day fresh! Keep me from stupid sins, from thinking I can take over your work; then I can start this day sun-washed, scrubbed clean of the grime of sin. These are the words in my mouth; these are what I chew on and pray. Accept them when I place them on the morning altar, O God, my Altar-Rock, God, Priest-of-My-Altar. (Psalm 19:12-14, MSG)

Praying God's Blessing for My Grown Child

I will lift up my eyes to the mountains; from where shall my help come? My help comes from the LORD, who made heaven and earth. He will not allow your foot to slip; He who keeps you will not slumber. Behold, He who keeps Israel will neither slumber nor sleep. The LORD is your keeper; the LORD is your shade on your right hand. The sun will not smite you by day, nor the moon by night. The LORD will protect you from all evil; He will keep your soul. The LORD will guard your going out and your coming in from this time forth and forever. (Psalm 121, NASB)

Blessings Now

- Adjust your vision by applying a new lens. Rather than regarding the measure of your parenting successes and failures according to how many of your expectations your child has or hasn't reached, turn your attention toward treasuring your relationship.

- Confirm your intentions. *Write and then throw out* a good-bye letter to your idealized grown child—the dreamed-of person you once imagined your son or daughter would be at this point in his or her life; *write and keep* a second letter for your private reference, describing your adult child as he or she actually is today and affirming as many details as you can about the God-given gifts and attributes you see in your grown child. Finally, *write and send* a third letter containing meaningful words of loving encouragement to your son or daughter.

- Get more understanding of your grown child's likes and interests. Join him or her for a movie, sporting event, or concert that you wouldn't normally attend, and then go out together afterward for coffee, dinner, or dessert.

- Think about your worry habit, if you have one, and how it affects your relationship with God, your heart, and your family. Look up some passages in the Bible that carry the warnings "Do not fret," "Have no anxiety," and "Don't worry." Consider the reasons why worry doesn't work. Name a specific area in your grown child's life (beliefs, work habits, relationships, health, finances, etc.) that you will actively avoid worrying about from now on. Replace worry with prayer.

- Practice forgiveness. Draw closer to Christ and rest in His love when you encounter feelings of loss, sadness, or anger about your imperfect relationship with your grown child—longing not only for *what has been* but also *what might have been*. Actively apply this strategy whenever you're tempted toward perfectionistic or negative thinking in your relationship.
- Express your gratitude for your son or daughter in a visible way. Leave a voice mail with kind words of appreciation; suggest doing something together if you live nearby—such as walking at the park, dining at a favorite restaurant, attending a church function, or having him or her over for a meal— offer to babysit; send a gift card in a thank-you note; show your care for your adult child's spouse; help out with something practical—pay for gas and an oil change, some groceries, or a hair salon or barber visit—mail an encouraging card with a photo from years past; and if you've been invited for a visit, make plans to go.

Wrap It Up, Give It to God

1. *Create a brief "for your eyes only" parenting autobiography.*
   Take into account the ways God has brought you through your
   family transitions so far, highlighting some of the benefits, hard-
   won experience, and wisdom you've gained along the way.

2. *Consider your parenting journey up to this point.* Record
   examples of the times when God's help and direction have been
   most clear to you, especially noting what you've learned when
   confronted with your imperfections and the limits of your control.

3. *Carry your concerns to the cross.* Review what you've written.
   Did anything come to your attention during this activity for
   which you especially need God's understanding, help, protection, and/or forgiveness? Are there any areas of concern about
   your adult child(ren) that have been weighing heavy on your
   heart? List these things on a note card, wrap it up, and give it
   to Christ in prayer, placing your burdens at the foot of His cross
   and leaving them there. Repeat as often as needed.

4. *Conclude with writing a prayer of petition and thanksgiving.* On
   a sheet of paper, express your desires for and gratitude to God
   regarding your grown child(ren). Keep this copy in a convenient
   private location for quick reference when you're tempted to
   worry or intervene unwisely.

CHAPTER THREE

Who's in Control?

Faith is to believe what you do not yet see; the reward for this faith is to see what you believe.

—AUGUSTINE OF HIPPO

When it comes to our children, we want to protect them from hurt or harm no matter what their ages. Due to our own experiences and education, we may understand better than they do the expected consequences of a particular route of action. But when we intervene unwisely, our benevolence is not a blessing.

My friend Amy and I recently discussed an ongoing dilemma she has been facing with her daughter Nina. "Before Nina was married nine years ago," Amy told me, "we often got together for lunch, talked on the phone, dropped by each other's houses for coffee, and attended church activities together. Of course I expected and accepted that this would change to some degree once she married. What I didn't anticipate is that she would marry a pastor from a church so different from our own."

"How is this affecting your relationship with your daughter now?" I asked.

"We rarely see each other anymore, and when we do, it's primarily at large family gatherings on holidays and special occasions. I understand that Nina doesn't have much time for one-on-one, casual get-togethers any longer, but it's more than that. When I first tried to arrange having coffee or lunch with my daughter early in her marriage to Ken, she said it would be best for her if we spent time together when her husband was also there. After having a brief conversation with her about it, I felt heartbroken when my beliefs about God were the reason Nina gave for her reluctance to continue getting together."

"Have you talked with Ken about this to better understand where they're both coming from?" I wondered aloud.

"I've periodically brought it up, but nothing has really changed," Amy responded. "I never pictured when my daughter was growing up that she would marry someone with such strict beliefs about limiting contact with people outside his denominational affiliation, including her mom."

Another friend of ours is grappling with the choices and priorities of his grown daughter Shannon. The last time he was in town for a visit, Derek shared openly with Dave and me about his daughter: "Sherry and I see Shannon a few times a year. Frequently she has a new boyfriend whom we meet while we're there, and he's usually quite a few years younger than she is.

"At thirty-four, our daughter concentrates her time and energy more on her career than on her personal relationships. She says she doesn't care if she gets married and has children, so dating someone much younger than she is makes a lot of sense to her. Given our family history—our four children, our long-term marriage, and living in this house here for more than forty years—Shannon's choices aren't easy for us to understand or relate to."

However disagreeable to us a possible outcome of our adult child's choices may be, consequences ultimately are a powerful remedy—one of the primary means of God's holy help. What is more, now that our kids are grown, we cannot prescribe the course of their lives nor manage the events and experiences that come their way, by choice or otherwise.

I'll say it again (because I also need to keep repeating this for myself): *We cannot prescribe the course of their lives nor manage the events and experiences that come their way, by choice or otherwise.*

Even though we understand that it's totally impossible to predict at the moment our kids are born where their life journeys will lead them, our attempts at retaining a measure of parental control seem almost automatic, don't they?

We want to support our children in walking toward the best possible future. We want to spend time with them and hope they want to spend time with us. We want to prevent their suffering, of every kind. We want to retain a certain level of godlike influence, wielding power over the situations that can break their hearts, drain their checkbooks, and damage their bodies. We want to give them a peaceful and pain-free life, where sin is rendered powerless and salvation is assured.

So, given that we already know we can't have everything we want, and being the self-motivated humans that we are, we yearn for the next best thing: *control.*

As my friend Pat shared with me, "I know I can't make my children's choices for them, because that's not my responsibility. I realize that healthy boundaries require constant self-restraint. But when I think there's going to be pain or failure involved, I suddenly want to step in and start trying to fix things."

And as my friend Beth told me at lunch recently, "I wish I knew

> *Do you trust God's good plans and purposes in the lives of your adult children, no matter what the circumstances look like? Do you believe that His redemptive work in your family doesn't change day to day?*

what lies ahead. Then I could just be prepared for it and figure out what to do! I really don't like not knowing what may happen next."

Something We All Struggle With

I wouldn't be writing this book today if I believed in my own power to be the perfect parent—or at least a perfectly wonderful one. Perhaps you can relate when I say I've tried everything I can think of to be the kind of mom I always wanted to have. Scratch that. I've tried *really hard* to be the kind of mom I always wanted to have.

My mom, like yours, did some things right—far more than a few, in fact. But she wasn't perfect. And the times in my life when I wished she could have understood me better, apologized when needed, been less defensive, seen who I was more clearly, accepted me as is, kept healthy boundaries, and heard my words well and often, minus projecting her own values and ideas, can't be reclaimed and relived. Nor can I return to those moments when it would have been best if I had done all of these things at various times for her.

No, my mother and main role model in the annals of parenting history wasn't perfect, and neither was I her perfect daughter. She failed to love me perfectly. I failed to love her perfectly. But eventually I came to understand that the sum total of our imperfect love for each other was more than enough for both of us.

It's such a relief to say this to you because, as fellow parents of adult children, I know you know what I'm talking about regardless of how our parents raised us and what our grown children are doing with their lives these days.

None of us are perfect, and that's okay. Our imperfect love is enough.

Stop! Look! Listen!

When you talk to your grown children, do you have a tendency to criticize, instruct, offer helpful hints, or make suggestions about how to do things differently? If so, try attending to what you say with an ear toward hearing your own words with third-party objectivity. Stop, take a look at yourself, and listen to what you're saying.

Consider how often your son or daughter may be hearing in your words or tone of voice one of these unspoken messages:

"I'm the parent, and you're not."

"I know, and you don't."

"I can think this through, and you can't."

"Wisdom rests in the heart of one who has understanding," we read in Proverbs 14:33 (NASB). Value the kind of understanding that invites others to grow in wisdom. Remember how you felt when your own parents respected and accepted your adult choices, or when they didn't; reflect on the mutually supportive ways you interact with your friends and peers; and offer your support by asking good questions that encourage your adult children to develop and mature in their own faith, beliefs, ideas, and coping skills.

Stop criticizing and correcting your adult children.

Look at how they respond to what you're saying.

Listen to yourself as well as to your grown children.

Adjusting Our Expectations

How could we possibly see at the beginning of our parenting experience the opportunities and challenges we and our adult kids would
eventually encounter? Among my friends and in my family (and
more than likely yours, too), our adult children have experienced and
celebrated a wide range of personal successes. It's what we haven't
seen coming that most often has led us to rely even more deeply
on God while discovering new dimensions of His love and grace.
These previously unimaginable life circumstances, and more, have
included . . .

Infertility	Marital conflict
Acute illness	Physical disability
Pregnancy complications	War injury
Incarceration	Unplanned pregnancy
Bipolar disorder	Cancer
Unemployment	Divorce
Child-custody dispute	Bankruptcy
Sexual promiscuity	Social withdrawal
Loneliness	Suicide
Loss of a child	Post-traumatic stress disorder
Substance abuse	Prolonged family dependence
Undesired singleness	Depression
Homelessness	Rape
Cult involvement	Unbelief
Gambling addiction	Eating disorders

Maybe you can identify with this list, or maybe you'd like to
add to it. The fact is that no matter what your family and mine
encounter over the years, we face a certain degree of adjustment regarding our expectations, whether the gap between what we want

for our grown children and what they experience is small (trivial to the point that we can say our kids have exceeded our hopes) or substantial (big enough to challenge our ability to comprehend their past or present life circumstances).

In time, this much is definitely true for *all* of us: There are some things we wish were different and some things we'd like to change about our grown children, as well as about ourselves, if we could.

No Simple Answers

In spite of how much we love our grown kids, we won't like everything that happens in their lives. We won't approve of all they say and do. We won't know how to respond to them in every situation, every single time. And we won't find simple answers to our toughest questions concerning their past or current choices and life circumstances. (And our grown children may feel the same way regarding us.)

Like it or not, this fact of life will always remain true: Our dreams are ours, not necessarily the dreams of our adult children. Our desires do not determine their choices.

Remember, our parents didn't agree with or appreciate every single one of our choices either. Let's be completely clear here: Did we do everything our moms and dads wanted, in exactly the way they expected, without ever causing our parents heartache, worry, irritation, or disappointment in the process? Of course we didn't. Did we choose to make wise changes after facing the consequences that came with some of our least favorable choices? We certainly did—and hopefully, our children will too.

Confronted with our myriad imperfections and the unforeseen

scenarios that can suddenly test the limits of our endurance, in each situation we have a choice concerning how we'll react as we allow our adult children time to learn and mature, as every wise and patient parent chooses to do.

As we breathe deeply and step back—not once or twice but numerous times—where will we turn for wisdom, patience, and relief? How can we find the strength to be faithful in our relationships with our adult children, allowing God to lead us to a compassionate understanding of their choices and wise acceptance of their

Judith and Sarah

It had been quite some time since I had seen Judith. Though our correspondence had mostly consisted of Christmas cards, as we sat down over coffee, it was only a few minutes before the comforting familiarity of our time-tested friendship reemerged.

Before long, the conversation turned toward the latest family updates: living locations, work assignments, graduations, the arrival of two grandchildren, and numerous upcoming celebrations.

"There's one more thing," my friend said, looking at me over the top of her trifocal lenses. "Jim and I are still coming to terms with it. We blamed ourselves at first. Didn't want people in our church to know."

I nodded and put my coffee cup down on the table, listening with quiet concern.

"Sarah isn't interested in dating men. Never has been, as you probably remember," explained Judith. "Still plays tennis competitively. She said she'd been afraid for years to tell us about her sexual preference for women, concerned that we would be angry with her and ashamed of her lifestyle."

need to assume responsibility for their lives?

Right now you may be thinking you'll never have the kind of relationship with your adult child that other parents seem to have with their grown kids—the kind of mutually rewarding, adult-to-adult bond you've always imagined you would have with your son or daughter.

Perhaps your adult child is struggling with one or many things on the list of challenges I mentioned earlier, as my own children have. Maybe your son or daughter simply isn't interested in being

"How did you feel when she shared this with you?" I asked.

"Honestly, Debra, it didn't surprise us at all. But that doesn't mean it has been easy," Judith admitted. "Jim and I entered counseling— which I can't recommend highly enough, if your therapist is a good fit—and that was a huge help. As long as we kept blaming ourselves, we couldn't see and accept Sarah, regardless of whether we agree with her choices or not. One of the most painful parts of all this has come through the harsh reactions of some of our friends."

"I understand how difficult that can be," I reassured her. "Where are things now?"

"We're learning how to love our children with greater understanding and compassion. We've stated our position; Sarah knows where we stand—and that her choices don't determine her value to us. Our love for our daughters and sons is nonnegotiable."

"Sounds to me like you appreciate more than ever the magnitude of God's grace, Judith. Just think where you and I would be today without it."

What will I do with my disappointment and desire for control when my grown child needs help or is hurting? How, and with whom, will I safely express my questions, thoughts, and feelings?

close to you at present. You might not know where your grown child is, or how to reach out and talk to him or her even if you do.

Regardless of the reasons why, if you're currently facing concerns in your relationship with your adult child, you may feel discouraged, grief-stricken, cynical, angry, confused, or frustrated. My question to you is simply this: So where do you want to go from here?

Seeing and Accepting

Though the number of events and experiences we cannot control and didn't cause in our adult children's lives may be much larger than we'd like to acknowledge, accepting the reality of our personal finiteness—along with daily trusting God's good plans and purposes for ourselves and our children—is our ongoing responsibility.

As we surrender to God our longing for control, opening our hearts to seeing and accepting our adult children as they really are rather than looking at them and their life circumstances as we ideally want them to be, our ability to love and forgive and bless them grows. Knowing that the way our grown children's lives appear at any particular moment in time is a single, temporary snapshot, that the pleasure or pain they feel today is only one small part of God's much larger design for their lives, encourages us to keep adjusting and enlarging our perspective.

On days when it's tempting to forget this, the following list can help to bring a certain measure of clarity:[1]

The Personal Characteristics, Choices, and Circumstances That I Can't Change or Control in My Grown Child's Life

- Personality and temperament
- Emotional, social, and spiritual growth
- Passions, preferences, and personal tastes
- Health and safety status
- Aptitudes, skills, and abilities
- Conversion and devotion to Christ
- Living location and environment
- Vocational and relationship choices
- Life goals, desires, and aspirations
- Level of career achievement
- Financial and social status
- State of happiness and emotional well-being
- Use of gifts and talents
- Spiritual beliefs and practices
- Size, appearance, and fitness level
- Decisions to engage in healthy or unhealthy habits: diet, exercise, smoking, alcohol or drug use, overworking, overspending, etc.
- Political affinities and affiliations
- Childbearing and childrearing preferences
- Peer-group and social-network choices

As you move forward to find peace, and perhaps a measure of reconciliation in your relationship with your grown child, it will mean honestly facing your feelings and attitudes toward him or her and asking God to help you surrender to Him the hurt and the guilt.

You might benefit from enlisting the support of trusted friends, and perhaps a family counselor. It may also be valuable for you to keep a journal about your relationships with each of your adult children, in which you can write down your thoughts, memories, feelings, and reflections during this process.

Ask God to help you identify and understand your fears and concerns, as well as any hurt and guilt you're carrying, regarding your grown children. Confess your wrongs, seek and accept Christ's forgiveness and grace, and move forward in the confidence that God is faithful to forgive you (see 1 John 1:9).

Let's not allow our grown children's choices and behavior to smash our God-given identity and self-esteem. It's never helpful to either parent or child if we forget who *we* are. Tearing down ourselves doesn't help anyone—least of all our grown children, who continue to benefit from our acceptance and understanding.

Those of us who are married will find that protecting our marriage bond from the effects of our adult children's stress will require extra care and attention. Taking the high ground will mean finding the time that's needed to talk with our spouse about what we're thinking and feeling; respecting his or her point of view on what's happening without imposing our own; choosing not to point fingers, demean, or criticize; discussing what to do together in response; and offering our love and support to each other along the way.

Those of us who are single will benefit from the encouragement of understanding friends and mentors who listen without making judgments about what our adult children are going through. Such well-weathered traveling companions know how to offer their perspective wisely, enhancing our ability to think and see things clearly. Whether married or single, we also need safe outlets for refreshment and relaxation in the midst of whatever may be going on.

With Christ at the center of our lives, and surrounded by a caring community of His design and our choice, we'll see our grown children differently—not as the source of our meaning or the measure of our success, but as God's own unique, flawed, imperfect individuals, who, just like us, are patiently, tenderly, wisely, unfailingly loved by our Father in heaven.

Words to Remember

- Show me your ways, O LORD, teach me your paths; guide me in your truth and teach me, for you are God my Savior, and my hope is in you all day long. (Psalm 25:4-5)
- Trust in the LORD with all your heart and do not lean on your own understanding. In all your ways acknowledge Him, and He will make your paths straight. (Proverbs 3:5-6, NASB)
- God is in charge of deciding human destiny. Who do you think you are to meddle in the destiny of others? (James 4:12, MSG)

Real Adults Share Their Stories

When I was in my early twenties, after I had told my mom and dad on several occasions that I didn't want them treating me like I still was in high school anymore, they suddenly seemed to become a lot smarter. I'm not sure how it happened—maybe they talked to someone or read something—but for whatever reason, I remember there was a major change for the better.

They asked me what I expected of them as parents now that I was older. This was huge because they'd never asked me anything like that before.

A few weeks after we talked about what I felt I still needed from them, I asked them what they expected from me. We were able to talk it through, and we reached some compromises on both sides.

One thing my dad said made a lot of sense. He said that "a good relationship isn't necessarily an easy or smooth relationship, with no real work required and without any ups or downs." He also told me his hope was "to keep the good connection between us growing with God's help." This meant a lot to me.

I really appreciate that my parents are making the effort to understand me and help me understand them.

—Grant

For Personal Reflection

1. When facing loss, disappointment, or unmet expectations related to my grown child, I find hope in believing . . .
2. Honoring and respecting God's gifts as uniquely expressed in my grown child's life can best be done by . . .
3. When I read the list of "Personal Characteristics, Choices, and Circumstances That I Can't Change or Control in My Grown Child's Life," I think about . . .

Prayers

Praying God's Blessing for My Family
And now, Master GOD, being the God you are, speaking sure words as you do, and having just said this wonderful thing to me, please, just one more thing: Bless my family; keep your eye on them always. You've already as much as said that you would, Master GOD! Oh, may your blessing be on my family permanently! (2 Samuel 7:28-29, MSG)

Praying God's Blessing for My Grown Child
May all the gifts and benefits that come from God our Father, and
the Master, Jesus Christ, be yours. (1 Corinthians 1:3, MSG)

Blessings Now

- Have a one-on-one conversation with your son or daughter.
  If it has been awhile since you've really talked with each
  other, start out with five minutes; in the next few weeks,
  aim for fifteen, and then eventually you may enjoy talking
  together for thirty minutes or longer.
- Given the wide range of crises and changes, large and small,
  that can come up as a part of living, aim to bless your son or
  daughter with your love, respect, and support while he or she
  learns indispensable life lessons. Recognize that you're not
  responsible for the consequences associated with your grown
  child's adult choices. You may also find it helpful to use some
  of these strategies recommended by real parents:
  - Give your advice when your son or daughter asks
    you for it.
  - Think before you talk.
  - Keep the lines of communication open.
  - Choose not to be defensive.
  - When necessary, clarify your concerns.
  - Ask for what you need and want.
  - Learn new life lessons rather than holding on to
    past failures and mistakes.
  - In a conflict, concentrate on finding the solution.
  - Resolve that your long-term relationship is more
    important than a short-term disagreement.

- Work toward positive outcomes instead of winning.
- Withstand shock, loss, disappointment, and hurt without getting stuck and becoming immobilized.
- Find the support and counsel you need when you need it.
- If your son or daughter tells you that he or she failed or fell short and asks your forgiveness, for-give—and avoid referring to the incident again.
- Value your adult child's highest good as your top priority.

• Refuse to be manipulated by blame or guilt as you seek God's help and direction today and in the future. Rest in God's grace with gratitude for new beginnings. Slow down. Evaluate your need for spiritual rest and nourishment. Cre-ate ample space and time for savoring God's Word.

• If you say or do something that bothers or upsets your adult child, apologize appropriately and promptly.

Stepping Back, Moving Forward

Take a Step Back

1. What do I see when I look at my relationship with my grown child?

2. Does my view allow me to identify the obstacles standing in the way of letting go?

3. Am I willing to make an honest assessment of the path ahead?

4. What or who will most help me look clearly at my current role and responsibilities concerning my adult child?

Survey the Situation

1. What's going on in my relationship with my adult child?

2. Do I genuinely recognize and respect my grown child's adulthood?

3. How am I contributing to my grown child's dependency on and/
   or independence from me?

4. If I've identified a specific area in our relationship I want to
   change, am I trying to sort things out or resolve it by myself? If
   so, where will I find trusted counsel and support?

Gain Insight into Unhealthy Patterns

1. What are my expectations regarding my grown child?

2. How do I respond when my expectations aren't met?

3. Have my adult child and I developed an unhealthy pattern of
   relating? Why does this keep happening?

4. In what ways, if any, do I avoid taking responsibility for the part I
   play in contributing to this unhealthy relationship pattern?

Recognize the Need for Change

1. What are my fears and concerns regarding my grown child?

2. How do I respond to my grown child's needs for separateness and connection?

3. Where is change in our relationship most needed?

4. Am I willing to make this change? What next steps am I willing to take?

Acknowledge Guilt

1. What, if anything, have I done (or not done) as a parent that I haven't sought and/or accepted God's forgiveness for?

2. Where is my sense of guilt concerning my grown child coming from? Am I or am I not at fault?

3. In what ways does guilt lead me into taking responsibility for my grown child's hurts, disappointments, or circumstances?

4. What steps do I need to take to release my guilt about the things I've said and done (or failed to say and do)?

Move Forward

1. Which new choices and behaviors will best support my adult child's need for appropriate separateness and closeness?

2. What changes do I need to make that will encourage my grown child to bear responsibility for his or her own choices, feelings, and circumstances?

3. How, where, and when will I place healthy boundaries between us?

4. How, where, and when will I make available my support and understanding?

PART II

The Blessings: Leaving Our Legacy

The eyes of all look expectantly to You, and You give them their food in due season. You open Your hand and satisfy the desire of every living thing. The LORD is righteous in all His ways, gracious in all His works.

—PSALM 145:15-17, NKJV

Some things work suddenly and are seen; others, such as the life of a seed, work slowly and silently.

—OSWALD CHAMBERS

CHAPTER FOUR

The Blessings
of Letting Go . . .
and Staying Connected

*Give your children up to God. It is
utterly safe to place your children in
God's sure hands.*

—John White

"Don't worry. I'll get this for you."

"Come on over. Our house is your house."

"Here's a twenty. I know you can use it right now."

"I want to know how you're doing. Call me again later."

As parents with grown children, we find these statements naturally familiar—sincere offers of solace and support for our grown children. But given the bigger picture of our adult-to-adult relationships, our words can also have an impact via an unspoken invitation: *Please keep relying on me . . . You're not grown up yet . . . I don't think you're doing so well . . . Let me take care of you.* The meaning depends on the need that exists, on either side, at any given moment.

Say, for example, a grown son stops by on his way to church to say hello to his parents and have a cup of coffee with them. As he leaves, his dad hands him money to help cover the expense of filling up his gas tank. Or perhaps an adult daughter calls in sick to work and then calls her mom, who makes a pot of homemade vegetable soup, which she later drops off at her daughter's nearby apartment, along with several over-the-counter remedies.

By giving his son the money, what did the dad get? In making the get-well delivery, whom has the mom helped?

If only the world were a kinder, easier, unbroken place, explaining these two scenarios could indeed be reduced to a simple, straightforward formula such as $1 + 1 = 2$. Letting go of our grown kids while staying connected with them would be a walk in the park, a breeze, with zero bumps and hazards on the road ahead. We would give wisely and unselfishly with clear consistency—and only when and where our actions would be most helpful.

We wouldn't want in any way whatsoever to retain our authority and control along the journey. It would be easy to simply and humbly step aside, and the feelings of guilt, grief, failure, anger, disappointment, shock, spite, pride, apathy, fear, burnout, or frustration that we sometimes encounter would disappear. We'd know how to perfectly handle every situation and balance the equation every single time without once getting in the way of our child's ongoing maturation (or our own). With no obstacles before us, we'd keep moving ahead by seeing, accepting, and loving our adult children as they truly are.

What's more, the son in our story would definitely use the money his dad gave him for gas, not a carton of unfiltered cigarettes, and the daughter lying in her bed at one o'clock in the afternoon would in fact have the flu, not a hangover, as she sipped a cup of her mom's fresh-from-the-garden soup.

If only the world were a kinder, easier, unbroken place.

What We *Can* Do

In the moments when we may wish we could more easily make everything better with a little cash or chicken soup, here's what we *can* do: We can bless our adult children by letting go of everything we cannot do for them and by depending on God's help and direction in our new ways of staying connected.

As grown children ourselves, we have a clear vantage point that allows each of us to observe how our parents birthed us into our adulthood: When did they first see and accept us as adults? In what ways did our moms and dads stop treating us like kids—positively or negatively, wisely or unwisely, too soon or too late—that resulted in our assuming a broader sense of self-responsibility? How do our mothers' and fathers' influence and generosity (or lack thereof) still affect us?

Pause for a moment to think about your life. Observe where you're situated right now in light of where you once thought you'd be at this point in your life. Consider the possibilities about where your life may still take you. If you add what you see to your parents' plans and expectations for you, what do you catch sight of when picturing your life story so far? Have there been some surprises?

What did we learn from our parents in the past that is helping or hindering us from letting go of and staying connected with our adult children today?

In time, our grown children's adulthood will confront them with the same questions about their lives that you and I have had the decades-long privilege of considering: *Who am I? Why am I here? Where am I going? When will I get there? Is God real? Who is Jesus? How do I know? Is there life after death? Do heaven and hell exist and, if so, who goes where? If God loves us, why does He allow us to be exposed to pain and temptation?*

Knowing that the world in which our sons and daughters are learning to survive isn't quite the same as when we grew up confronts us with our own set of yet-to-be-answered questions. Add to this our sincere hope, and the understandable pressure we feel, that our grown children ideally will prosper—that they will follow Christ, graduate from college, live with moral integrity, remain physically and mentally fit, earn a good income, and establish their own healthy marriages and families—and it's not surprising why we may find it harder to let go and stay connected wisely than to simply "help out."

Truth be told, what we most want for our grown children— their ultimate safety, security, and salvation—we cannot give them. What we can provide them, however, is our steady recognition, acceptance, and respect as we love them and set the necessary limits. We can let them go *and* stay connected, not simply one or the other. Finding a resilient balance between a host of essential needs redefines and reshapes our relationship with them in mutually beneficial ways.

For our bonds to remain whole and healthy, a number of our past parental behaviors will fall away as new relational patterns emerge

Sharon, Paul, and Amanda

It often seems in retrospect that we see more clearly what the best course of action might have been with our grown children.

Take, for example, Sharon and Paul's decision to pay for their daughter Amanda's wedding. They had strong reservations about Nick, Amanda's previously divorced fiancé, but after discussing their concerns with their daughter, they accepted her decision and offered their full support.

During Amanda and Nick's engagement, more concerns came up. Sharon and Paul recommended counseling and stepped out of the way while the couple worked through their issues. At several points, Amanda was ready to break up with Nick but then reconciled with him. Through it all, Sharon and Paul gave their daughter and her fiancé their spiritual, emotional, and financial support, including covering the cost of the wedding.

A few years after the wedding, Amanda and Nick's marriage legally ended after he entered into an intimate relationship with a co-worker. He married again within a month and became a father only four months afterward. Later, Sharon and Paul discovered on their credit report that Nick had used their personal information to apply for a loan.

"Looking back," Sharon says, "I wonder if accepting our daughter's decision and speaking the truth in love to her about our concerns before she married was enough. Perhaps the expression of our care for Amanda would have had a different impact if we had encouraged her to make sound choices but withheld our financial support."

Sharon admits, "I still wonder whether helping Amanda ended up hurting her in the long run. If we had backed her up and refused to pay for her dream wedding when she expressed reluctance about marrying Nick, would it have made any difference?"

that recognize, support, and respect our children's adult status. It's our responsibility to continue loving them wisely—most especially, perhaps, when their real-life, broken-world experiences don't coincide with our highest hopes and best plans for them.

Now, we find ourselves in the position of shielding our adult children not so much from themselves as from our own fears and frustrations concerning their lives.

"If you become a necessity to someone else's life, you are out of God's will," Oswald Chambers cautions us. "Over and over again, we try to be amateur providences in someone's life. We are indeed amateurs, coming in and actually preventing God's will and saying, 'This person should not have to experience this difficulty.'"[1]

Clearly, we aren't sovereign over our grown children, just as we aren't sovereign over ourselves. But that just may be what we're tempted to believe when we start thinking we can somehow ensure or secure our adult son's or daughter's salvation, sanctification, and success.

As we discover sooner or later, letting go of our grown children while staying connected to them is about much more than focusing on our own plans and expectations. It's about opening our eyes to their adult identity, seeing what we can and cannot do, and entrusting their lives as well as ours to the one unfailing Father of us all.

Is there an area of my grown child's life that I'm involved in too much or too little? Am I having difficulty letting go because of something I need to stop supporting? Have I become detached because the difficulty lies in knowing how and where to stay connected? What will I do instead?

Too Much, Too Little, and Finding the Balance

"I'm concerned that the gap between what Sean and I have and what our kids have is growing wider," my friend Toni told me the other day. "They're now both over thirty, single, and struggling to make it financially. Neither of them has health insurance or retirement savings, owns a home, or is debt-free. Hayley is working full-time but said last week that she wants to move back in with us at the end of the month. After talking through her options with her, we agree this makes sense for the time being because she can't afford to pay her current bills."

Dave and I have felt this same concern at various times, as do millions of other parents whose grown children's standard of living isn't within reach of their parents' level of comfort. It matters to us when our sons and daughters can't afford to cover the costs of doctor's office visits, drug prescriptions, or safe housing. I wish I could say that it's always easy to figure out when and where our support is most needed—sometimes it is, sometimes it isn't, as you know.

In truth, letting go and staying connected *does* look different to those of us with grown children today than it did to our parents, for many reasons. According to a survey by Monster.com, the popular online job and talent search engine, approximately 52 percent of recent college graduates lived with their parents in 2010, up from 40 percent the previous year.[2] It isn't a surprising statistic given our nation's high unemployment rate and the fact that many college graduates today are saddled with an average student-loan debt of $20,000.[3] Consider also this recent report by the Pew Research Center:

[Thirteen percent] of parents with grown children say one of their adult sons or daughters has moved back home in

the past year. Social scientists call them "boomerangers"—
young adults who move in with parents after living
away from home. This recession has produced a bumper
crop.[4]

Given that our children's generation is poised to become "the
first in a century that is unlikely to end up better off financially" than
ours,[5] how will we wisely, generously, and compassionately respond?

Here are some examples of the kinds of material help we've provided our grown children and grandchildren since our first child
reached the age of eighteen more than twenty years ago:

- Food, clothing, gasoline, and educational assistance
- Health- and dental-care coverage
- Housing costs, including rent, security deposits, down
  payments, and repairs
- Telephone and utility service
- Plane tickets, car rentals, and hotels
- Furniture, appliances, and other household items
- Cars, including purchases, license tags, insurance, mainte-
  nance, and repairs
- Milestone-related expenses accompanying birthdays,
  weddings, graduations, and new baby arrivals
- Tax and legal fees
- Recreational equipment and memberships, such as city
  parks and recreation passes, YMCA, and Gymboree
- Moving expenses
- Emergency veterinary care
- Contributions to their employers (churches and nonprofit
  organizations)
- And, of course, cash

In addition, each of our daughters and sons has moved back into our home at least once, on a temporary or extended basis, since reaching adulthood. When our grown children have lived out of state, Dave and I have traveled to be with them during times of celebration, such as our daughter's wedding in Missouri, the birth of our first grandchild in Georgia, and our son's graduation in Colorado. In times of anguish—funerals, hospitalizations, divorce proceedings, and unexpected pregnancy loss—we have been there as well.

I haven't made a list like this until now, partly because I believe it's best to count the cost on the front end as much as possible, and partly because it hadn't occurred to me to make such a list. I share these things with you simply to say that Dave and I have been there and back as parents, perhaps a lot like you. We've made mistakes and learned a great deal along the way, as you also undoubtedly have. And for as long as we stay the course in loving our grown children, which I trust we—and you—will, I'm guessing that in our commitment to letting go and staying connected, we'll continue to venture into all manner of life-giving territory.

What We *Do* Know

If only we had known twenty years ago what we know now . . . Nevertheless, here's what we *do* know today:

1. Getting out of the way of our adult children's decisions means that we can choose to support their actions—or not.
2. Extending our acceptance to our adult children isn't dependent on extending to them our support and approval—we can offer our love to them without backing their personal choices.

3. If there is a clear reason for us to support our adult children's choices, they and we will likely benefit from our loving allowance and provision of this support.

4. If there is a clear reason for us not to support our children's choices, they and we will likely benefit from our loving refusal or withdrawal of this support.

5. We'll always benefit from asking and thinking through our answer to this question, before rather than after: *How will my parental care and support help and/or hinder my grown child in this situation?*

The blessing of letting go means moving away from carrying our earlier responsibility for setting limits on our children and moving into our present responsibility with regard to setting limits on ourselves. We know this because we learned it first by experience: Children move away from their parents in order to move closer to God. Accepting the necessary losses we incur along the way opens avenues of meaningful possibility for our future.

Put simply, since we're no longer in charge of our grown children's choices, we aren't responsible for the choices they make. We remain their parents, however, which requires wise discernment regarding how and where we will stay connected.

Thinking through—and, when appropriate, discussing—the following topics fosters the adult-to-adult relationship that is now our privilege to share with our grown children:

• *Advice.* Have they asked for it?

• *Visits.* How often, and for how long, do they prefer and expect that you will spend time with them?

• *Communication.* How often, and for how long, do they prefer and expect that you will talk and correspond?

• *Emotional support.* Are you offering your assistance because they desire it?

- *Financial help.* How much is too much? How little is too little?
- *Beliefs.* In what ways do your beliefs differ? Are there topics or activities they prefer you not discuss?
- *Lifestyle choices.* How much and how often are your thoughts, feelings, and actions influenced and affected by their current decisions?
- *Privacy.* Do you respect one another's privacy? How can you tell?
- *Intervention.* How will you determine when your intervention is and isn't needed?
- *Gifts.* Do they have preferences about the number, cost, and types of gifts you give?
- *Change.* Are you expecting that they will change rather than determining the changes you need to make and then moving ahead?
- *Growth.* Have they taken responsibility for their own physical, emotional, spiritual, and social health? Are you still carrying too much of the load?

Knowing the Difference

For Alan, welcoming his son Reid back home following his diagnosis with bipolar mood disorder provided more than a safe place for Reid to stay. Both father and son have had the opportunity to spend time talking and doing things together as adults, deepening their relationship and love for each other.

"For a long time," Alan said, "I regretted that Reid and I had missed out on developing much of a friendship before he left for college. His health crisis has given us the chance to get to know and appreciate each other through the counseling we've received and the time we spend together. I'm not sure how long he'll be living with us, but I'm not concerned about that right now. We have the space, and our house rules and weekly counseling visits go a long way toward keeping things going smoothly. Getting Reid stabilized is my priority for the time being."

For Kim, encouraging her daughter Jessica's well-being has given both of them a chance to grow in their relationship. "As a working mom, Jessie appreciated that I'm available to help out by caring for her children on days when she can't pick them up from school, wants to have time alone with her husband, or needs support on Saturdays while running errands. Being able to spend time with my granddaughters and at the same time provide this support for my daughter works out well for us all."

For Jill, re-evaluating her future in light of her parents' challenges and grown children's needs has allowed her greater freedom to put her faith into action. "My father had difficulty saving and investing, choosing instead to spend his money unwisely. He lived extravagantly, over the years spending a fortune on his own interests without apparently understanding or caring about how he might have made a difference in the lives of his wife, children, and grandchildren. Facing the impact of my father's example, forgiving him, and receiving God's forgiveness for the way I've judged him, have allowed me to change the way I view and manage money. So I've become smarter as well as more generous with my grown children."

Yes, we'll find ourselves doing a significant amount of letting go and staying connected with our grown children over the span of our lifetimes—with God's help "accepting the things we cannot change, changing the things we can, and seeking the wisdom we need, day by day, to know the difference," as the well-known prayer fittingly reminds us.

Are we ready to bless our grown children by letting go of whatever holds us back and staying involved where we can be of most benefit, especially in the areas where God is inviting us to trust Him more?

Through acknowledging God's care and guidance over our adult children's life choices, circumstances, and experiences, we can choose to open our hands and surrender to Him the fears, concerns, and anxieties to which we cling. In exchange, we'll receive a greater measure of joy and the insight gained in letting go . . . and staying connected.

Words to Remember

- We live by faith, not by sight. (2 Corinthians 5:7)
- But we have this treasure in jars of clay, to show that the surpassing power belongs to God and not to us. (2 Corinthians 4:7, ESV)
- [Then Jesus said,] "Come to me, all you who are weary and burdened, and I will give you rest. Take my yoke upon you and learn from me, for I am gentle and humble in heart, and you will find rest for your souls. For my yoke is easy and my burden is light." (Matthew 11:28-30)

Real Adults Share Their Stories

My mom and dad are generous parents. I'm able to count on them when needed. I know it hasn't always been easy for them, either. They encourage me to work and live independently, and they also extend their grace and understanding when things come up that I don't plan on. Both have been willing to ask how I'm doing at various times and respond with kindness when they know I've done my best to make ends meet and still come up short.

I hope to have children of my own someday. When and if I do, I hope I'll be the kind of parent to my kids that my parents have been to me.

—Luke

For Personal Reflection

1. I find myself most wanting to take responsibility for my grown child's choices when . . .
2. Believing that God knows my fears and frustrations as a parent allows me to . . .
3. Giving my grown child the blessing of my letting go and staying connected requires . . .

Prayers

Praying God's Blessing for My Family
Know this: GOD is God, and God, GOD. He made us; we didn't make Him. We're His people, His well-tended sheep. Enter with the password: "Thank You!" Make yourselves at home, talking praise. Thank Him. Worship Him. (Psalm 100:3-4, MSG)

Praying God's Blessing for My Grown Child
May my child call upon You, LORD, and may You answer him (or her); may You be with my child in trouble, may You deliver and honor my child. May You satisfy my child with long life and show him (or her) Your salvation. (Adaptation of Psalm 91:15-16)

Blessings Now

- Think about and identify the main ways you do and do not treat your son or daughter as an adult. Compare this list with the ways you treat adults who are not your child. After noting the differences, boost your maturing relationship by setting a limit on yourself that will be most beneficial for both you and your grown child.

- Recognize and respect your adult child's responsibility to decide what to do with his or her resources and relationships. If needed, ask your grown son or daughter, in turn, to recognize and respect your responsibility to make sound decisions concerning how you invest your time, money, and energy.

- Define the basic rules, big and small, that you believe play a necessary part in maintaining any adult-to-adult relationship. Apply these to your relationship with your grown child. (For example: I will respect the privacy of others, which means I won't just drop by for a visit; I'll always call first.)

- Discover your answer to this question: How and when may helping my son or daughter actually hurt him or her? Give to your adult child the blessing of your letting go in this area of his or her life. Support your grown child as he or she learns how to become an independent adult who can survive and thrive on his or her own. If one or more adult children are financially dependent upon and/or living with you, consider the following advice:
    - Talk with your spouse about the situation and/or consult with a trusted friend, adviser, or counselor. You've likely been offering your support because you believe your adult child needs it. Determine

how much you actually want and can afford to help, or whether you should help. Outline and examine the reasons why your grown child wants to live at home, if he or she requests to do so. Notice whether you feel guilty, afraid, or reluctant when you require your son or daughter to make even minimum financial contributions to his or her expenses (rent, food, etc.), and discern why you feel this way.

- Initiate a series of family meetings about money. Explain and discuss with your adult child the amounts you're spending monthly, including the cost of food, utilities, phone, property maintenance, insurance, clothing, and any cooking and cleaning services. Set clear limits. Require reasonable contributions and accountability. Use regularly scheduled meetings to cover money-related topics rather than bringing up a financial concern when you're tired, frustrated, or in the midst of a disagreement.

- Review and, if needed, re-evaluate your reasons for offering your support, such as reduced income, divorce, illness, legal or financial trouble, pregnancy, college attendance, job loss, temporary housing during relocation, single-parent support, developmental disability, or wanting your child to be near you. Discuss and decide how much of your support is currently necessary, as well as how much your adult child can reasonably afford to contribute to his or her expenses. If you're regularly providing any of life's basic necessities free of charge, perhaps your adult child doesn't yet understand the rough reality of the costs of living today.

Take a Closer Look

Consider and distinguish the differences between (a) connection and (b) enabling from the following list, identifying any areas in which you currently find it difficult to let go of your concerns for and about your grown child. Learn more about the enabling behaviors you may recognize in yourself. Use a variety of available resources and find caring support as you work toward making changes.

    a. I seek to understand and accept my grown child's behavior.

    b. I make excuses for my grown child's behavior.

    a. I express my confidence to my grown child about his or her problem-solving capability.

    b. I feel afraid for my grown child because I don't think my child can handle the relationship/situation that he or she is in.

    a. I trust that I'm doing enough for my grown child.

    b. I worry that I'm not doing enough for my grown child.

    a. I typically avoid doing for my grown child what he or she can do for himself or herself.

    b. I frequently do for my grown child what he or she can do for himself or herself.

    a. I offer my suggestions and recommendations with respect for my grown child's freedom to make up his or her own mind.

    b. I feel frustrated or angry when my grown child doesn't follow up on my suggestions and recommendations.

a. I recognize my grown child's behavior, attitudes, and situation as uniquely his or her own.
b. I see myself in my grown child's behavior, attitudes, and situation.

a. I choose to help my grown child out financially.
b. I owe it to my grown child to make arrangements for and/or help him or her financially.

a. It's my grown child's responsibility to find help and support.
b. It's my responsibility to find help and support for my grown child.

a. I pray for my grown child, surrender to God my concerns for his or her situation, and experience peace.
b. I spend a lot of time thinking and/or worrying about my grown child's situation.

a. I recognize when my grown child tries to manipulate me, and I call him or her out on it.
b. I realize my grown child sometimes manipulates me, and I hide my feelings about it.

a. I accept it as part of life when others are critical of my grown child, even though I may dislike it or disagree with them.
b. I get defensive when others are critical of my grown child, and I want them to change their viewpoint.

a. I consider my time, energy, budget, relationships, and personal responsibilities before deciding how and when I will help my grown child.

b. I help my grown child at an imbalanced cost to my time, energy, budget, relationships, and personal responsibilities.

CHAPTER FIVE

The Blessings of a Safe Place

Only when you are able to set your own boundaries will you be able to acknowledge, respect and even be grateful for the boundaries of others.
—HENRI J. M. NOUWEN

Recently I was flipping through the channels, looking for something interesting to watch on TV, when a popular home-organization program began. Interestingly, it featured a couple with grown children going through the clearing-out and cleaning-up process, with more than a little help from the show's undaunted host. One of the things that most stood out to me about the hour-long episode was what I'd call the visibility of the obvious—in this case, the way the vast amount of accumulated stuff was immediately apparent to any viewer. Yet, from the family's perspective, the towering stacked boxes, swollen plastic bags of unused clothes, and heaped household items that filled their living space weren't clearly evident. Why not?

Seen in a colorful close-up, their countless trophies, nursery-school drawings, baby clothes, report cards, vacation maps, holiday costumes, old toys, and well-marked cookbooks represented their shared history, a meaningful part of the past that they were understandably reluctant to shed.

As their mom urged them to keep heading for the trash bin, the two grown daughters continued piling things in the bins marked "TO KEEP." Finally, when it became clear that the home-improvement process wasn't going to go anywhere without the daughters understanding what needed to happen next, the show's host said something like, "Okay, that's enough. As I said earlier, you can keep the most important things. Everything else needs to be given away or discarded. I can see you're having difficulty dealing with your family's need to move ahead. Let's turn the cameras off and talk about this."

The main issue was there, staring them right in the face, blocking their view of what their lives could be like once the arduous three-day task of downsizing was finished. Clearly, the daughters had their reasons for clinging to the past rather than reaching toward new possibilities for their future. I loved seeing them experience the freedom that blossomed from their willingness to grow and learn.

Now that the years of raising our young families are behind us, you and I have officially entered a "What stays in and what stays out?" personal downsizing era of our own.

Let me say this up front: When it comes to completely figuring out what an empty-nest kind of safe place looks like, I and every parent I know are in the "still learning" phase of the growing-up process. Moving out of the "Let's all stay close and safe now, shall we?" abode that once seemed as if it would last for good clearly doesn't happen overnight, let alone in three days flat. And because the mature-adult version of home we now find ourselves living in is significantly smaller than our previous multi-family-member one, it can be confusing where the boundaries of our new lives belong.

In most cases, our grown children no longer share the same everyday life space we do. Whether or not we reside in the same house or go to the same church or vote for the same political party, whether our full-time job previously involved being a stay-at-home parent or working in an occupation outside of the home, the safe place that second-stage parenting calls us to move into requires new personal boundaries. It's going to thrive only if we're willing to put a beautiful brand-new door on it, accompanied by the blessing of a good lock without a common household key. By necessity, it's time for our adult children to move out of the safe place we now occupy and are responsible for.

Even though I know this is true, when it comes to my grown children, my heart can take on heaps of care on their behalf, crowding out my opportunity, and theirs, to develop in new directions.

Too often I want to plunge in and fix the things in my grown children's lives that only God can fix. I give advice when listening would be better, say yes when saying no could produce greater growth, dispute their need for privacy when I want to know something that isn't any of my business, believe that I know what they should say, think, or do when I disagree with their choices, and so on.

As it turns out, one of the best home-organization coaches around asks the questions about downsizing that also happen to be quite effective for enhancing the shape and style of our heart's empty-nest design:

- What is my vision for the phase of life in which I now reside?

- What am I not seeing in my life that will benefit from my clearing out and cleaning up?
- What do I want to put in and keep out of my empty nest?

Take a moment to do a quick mental walk-through of the personal space you occupy. Survey your life's physical, emotional, and spiritual condition. What areas most need your attention? Is your heart currently cluttered with cares that aren't your burden to be carrying? Have you piled on any responsibility for your grown child's life that isn't yours to manage? How will you downsize your safe place so you can provide more room for God's plans and purposes for your and your child's lives?

Hold On or Move On?

It took time, effort, and education to acquire the necessary habits that shaped our daily lives as families during the years when we were responsible for our children's well-being. So it makes complete sense that moving on from, rather than holding on to, these familiar patterns takes time, effort, and education too.

This daily learning experience involves an ongoing willingness to keep our eyes open for the good things ahead as we acquire fresh wisdom. It's also a step-by-step education in how to say yes or no while figuring out when we're being asked to give more than what is wise for us to give and determining what is best and most helpful for us to offer.

As my friend Tami told me, "It never ceases to amaze me. When it comes to my kids, somehow I don't necessarily feel the need to live by the rules that guide my other adult relationships. I even opened my son's mail the other day—something I wouldn't think of doing with any of my friends. Because Larry owes me money and I didn't trust him to tell me the truth about how much he was getting back for his federal income-tax refund, I too quickly justified my behavior."

Charles acknowledges his own learning process in creating a safe place in which mutual love and respect can thrive with his grown children: "I most often overstep my bounds as a dad when my grown children ask for my help and I say okay, not because I've thought it through, but because I don't like what's happening, such as the time I gave our son permission to move back home when he could have afforded to rent a one-room apartment in a less-than-ideal part of town."

He adds, "My understanding of what qualifies as necessary has recently started changing, though. I can see more clearly why and where I cross my children's boundaries, as well as my own—it usually happens when I try to prevent the consequences of their choices. While I'll always want my grown children to know they can count on me, the things I want them to count on me for are the things they can't do for themselves, not what they'll benefit from doing themselves."

Our hearts exist alongside and affect others. This seems to be one of the reasons we require healthy personal boundaries. "Keep and guard your heart with all vigilance and above all that you guard, for out of it flow the springs of life," the book of Proverbs advises (4:23, AMP).

Personal boundaries help us define what stays in and what stays out—who we are and who we are not; what we want and what we do not want; what we will do and what we will not do. Setting our

Susie and Sam

An important turning point in Susie's relationship with her grown child arrived one day a few years ago. Her son Sam needed help—money, a place to stay, some food, a shower.

This would have been no big deal for many parents and their sons in everyday circumstances. But Sam has a life-threatening disease. His alcoholism requires his parents to let go of taking care of him.

So Susie said no to her son.

After closing the front door with Sam still outside, some of Susie's old, familiar fears popped up: *What if Sam walks away and I never see him again? What if he won't listen and comes back? What if he doesn't stop drinking? What if he ends up in jail? What if he can't find the help he needs? What if he dies?* These thoughts immediately began crowding out her conviction that if she had said yes, it would have produced greater harm than setting a new boundary in their relationship.

It had required so much time, energy, money, effort, education, support, counseling, prayer, and lost sleep for Susie to be able to say that one word and truly mean it.

No.

"When I heard Sam walk away," Susie recalls, "I didn't know what the outcome would be. I honestly couldn't tell whether my decision would help or hurt.

"Sitting at the kitchen table, I asked God for His wisdom as the tears ran down my cheeks. Passages from the Psalms drew my attention away from the turmoil, toward Jesus's comfort and rest.

"But what if Sam dies, Lord?" Susie prayed.

Her heart's toughest question—and her desire to prevent this

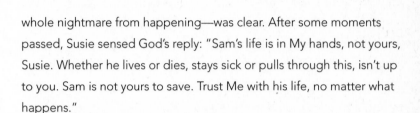

whole nightmare from happening—was clear. After some moments passed, Susie sensed God's reply: "Sam's life is in My hands, not yours, Susie. Whether he lives or dies, stays sick or pulls through this, isn't up to you. Sam is not yours to save. Trust Me with his life, no matter what happens."

Sam is not yours to save. Trust Me with his life, no matter what happens.

Susie and her husband, Vince, prayed together and individually, along with the close friends and family members she called for additional support. A few hours later, Sam came back to their house. By that time, Vince was home from work. When he saw his impaired son sitting outside looking as if he was ready to pass out, Vince called the police. This may sound like an over-reaction, but as it turned out, the call may have saved Sam's life.

No parent wants to be the one to turn his or her child over to the authorities. Susie knows because she and Vince had bailed Sam out before—on several occasions. For years they believed they could "handle" their son, change the course of his life, and get him back on track. Not true.

"Understanding and accepting the severity of Sam's disease and the parts we do and don't, can and can't play in his life, continues to be a step-by-step process," Susie notes. "I sometimes wish I could have all the answers, right now, without having to keep asking the same questions: How much? How little? Where? When? The alternative, though, would mean letting go of my son altogether, and dismissing my continuing need to rely on God's grace, strength, and help."

boundaries determines how we honor the safe place that separates who we are—what we think, feel, and do—from the thoughts, feelings, and actions of those around us. These choices make room for our ability to see, value, understand, and take responsibility for ourselves, and in turn allow us to value the unique expression of God's image in our adult children.

Decluttering and simplifying the personal space of our hearts, minds, and spirits can seem like a daunting task, without question. Defining with clear boundaries the safe place where we want and need to live so that we'll "be able to acknowledge, respect, and even be grateful for the boundaries of others," as Henri Nouwen expressed it, is a renovation project like no other. But the rewards make the effort required worth it! With God's help, the safe place that is being created with our willing cooperation—scaling back our earlier child-centered purpose in favor of the broader Christ-centered purpose God has planned for us in second-stage parenting—will bring to us and our children benefits today and in the years to come.

While we cannot create, direct, or control the changes taking place in our adult children's lives, it's our responsibility to learn to live with less worry and more peace, less fear and more grace, regardless of their choices and the consequences that follow. The wisdom we gain in the process will bless them, and us, as well.

When it comes to our grown children, for whom and for what are we now responsible? In what areas is their business any longer our business? How much do we give, say, do, tell, warn, offer, advise, suggest, correct, ignore, or try to prevent from happening?

Safe and Sound

In this constantly changing world we live in, our Savior bids us to walk with Him in newness of life. There is no mistaking His wondrous intention. He is our safe place.

Whatever the out-of-bounds craving that anyone in our families may be facing, the most important help we need is available, at all times and in all places:

> For we do not have a high priest who is unable to sympathize with our weaknesses, but one who in every respect has been tempted as we are, yet without sin. Let us then with confidence draw near to the throne of grace, that we may receive mercy and find grace to help in time of need. (Hebrews 4:15-16, ESV)

The sense of loss we encounter when our children leave us and the wounds we may have experienced earlier in our family relationships take time to heal. Filling our emptiness by doing too much for our grown children or trying harder to undo our past mistakes in an effort to prove we're worthy of our children's love won't produce the healthy outcome we desire. "We change our behavior when the pain of staying the same becomes greater than the pain of changing," Dr. Henry Cloud and Dr. John Townsend remind us. "Consequences give us the pain that motivates us to change."[1]

By coming to terms with the things we cannot change or control and don't like, approve of, or agree with in our grown children's lives, we can

- Accept that it's beyond our control to save or change our adult children.
- Express our concern as well as our love to our grown children.

> *Do I struggle with old or new hurts regarding my grown child? When I recall what I could have done differently two weeks or twenty years ago, have I surrendered my guilt to God and sought His healing for my heart?*

- State that we don't want our acceptance to be misinterpreted as an endorsement of our adult children's behavior.
- Surrender to God the things we cannot change or control, including our grown children's life choices, which we don't condone or support.

Without a doubt, absolutely, no question: We can't discover our grown children's best faith expression, earn their perfect job, orchestrate their ideal relationships, change their messy past, or arrange a pain-free future for them. *We cannot change them.*

But it doesn't stop there. By God's grace and with His Spirit's help, *we can change.* And along the way, our heart's capacity to love and accept our grown children will grow. First Peter 4:8 says, "Most of all, love each other as if your life depended on it. Love makes up for practically anything" (MSG).

Yielding our life to God and sharing the blessings of a safe place within His grace—actively depending on Christ from moment to moment while abiding in the refuge of His keeping—gives us the opportunity to surrender not only our life to the Lord but also our concerns about our grown children's welfare. As His followers, we find our identity and greatest joy in Someone beyond ourselves. By faith we believe that our heavenly Father is forming our character and identity in the image of His Son as we yield our lives to His remaking.

Choose how you will make your second-stage parenting way of life a safe place where you and your maturing family can thrive. What will you take out of your nest and leave behind? What do you want to keep from the past? What do you want to put in as you head into your future?

Words to Remember

- I can do everything God asks me to with the help of Christ who gives me the strength and the power. (Philippians 4:13, TLB)
- God can do anything, you know—far more than you could ever imagine or guess or request in your wildest dreams! He does it not by pushing us around but by working within us, his Spirit deeply and gently within us. (Ephesians 3:20, MSG)
- For God did not give us a spirit of timidity, but a spirit of power, of love and of self-discipline. (2 Timothy 1:7)

Real Adults Share Their Stories

My mom used to have a tendency to talk a lot, especially when she was worried about me or one of my sisters. I appreciated her care and concern, but she could quickly get on my nerves—too many questions! I didn't like hearing her go on about things that weren't really any of her business. Looking back, I think Mom didn't totally realize at the time the impact her worrying and running commentary had on the rest of us.

Things changed after my youngest sister left home for college. Mom went back to school, got her master's degree, and now does counseling part-time. She also teaches, travels, and mentors younger women. If she worries about me, I'm not aware of it.

In the past I was reluctant to talk much with Mom about my life because I didn't know how she was going to respond. I'm grateful she can listen now, and I consider her one of my best friends in the whole world. When something comes up in my life that I want someone to pray about, I call my mom.

—Sasha

For Personal Reflection

1. In taking responsibility for downsizing my safe place, I will place limits with my grown child in the areas where I have a tendency to . . .
2. Keeping my heart in Christ's safekeeping results when . . .
3. I most value the two-sided benefits and blessings of living within my boundaries when . . .

Prayers

Praying God's Blessing for My Family

May God, our very own God, continue to be with us just as he was with our ancestors—may he never give up and walk out on us. May he keep us centered and devoted to him, following the life path he has cleared, watching the signposts, walking at the pace and rhythms he laid down for our ancestors. (1 Kings 8:57-58, MSG)

Praying God's Blessing for My Grown Child

My response is to get down on my knees before the Father, this magnificent Father who parcels out all heaven and earth. I ask him to strengthen you by his Spirit—not a brute strength but a glorious inner strength—that Christ will live in you as you open the door and invite him in. And I ask him that with both feet planted firmly on love, you'll be able to take in with all followers of Jesus the extravagant dimensions of Christ's love. Reach out and experience the breadth! Test its length! Plumb the depths! Rise to the heights! Live full lives, full in the fullness of God. (Ephesians 3:14-19, MSG)

Blessings Now

- Take into account that all change brings opportunities and challenges.
- Ask yourself as often as needed, "How can I encourage, support, and help my grown child survive on his or her own?"
- Monitor and meet your basic needs for sleep, healthy food and exercise, spiritual encouragement, solitude, and Christian community. If you'd like additional support to promote your well-being, make an appointment with your health-care provider, pastor, or counselor to discuss positive strategies.
- Consider how you may be trying to fix your grown child. What have you been trying to control or change? Make two lists: On the first, write down the areas of your grown child's life you would most like to change or control, if you could. On the second, record your recent thoughts, behaviors, and attitudes that reveal or demonstrate your desires for your son or daughter and your frustrations regarding your inability to change or control him or her. Think through ways you can be a gracious influence instead of attempting to change your grown child. What will you do to change yourself?

- Stop rebuilding your grown child inside your head according to your own plans. Instead, build him or her up in reality:
  - Aim toward offering your love, acceptance, and understanding in place of criticism.
  - Steer away from offering suggestions for improvement.
  - Allow and encourage your grown child to speak for him- or herself.
  - Avoid assuming that you know what your adult child thinks, sees, believes, knows, understands, or feels.
  - Forgive your grown child for his or her limitations and ask God to forgive your own.
  - When your adult child is ready to talk to you, listen with your undivided attention.
  - Steer away from the temptation to interpret or represent your grown child's choices, convictions, ideas, and actions to others.
  - Refuse to disparage or become distracted by your grown child's behaviors and attitudes.
  - Make requests, rather than demands; respond rather than react.
  - Remember who you are and that your love comes from God.
  - Consider the truth behind what may seem an unfair criticism.
  - Don't retaliate—learn from what's happening instead.
  - Respect your adult child's ideas even when you disagree.
  - Stop comparing your adult child with anyone else.

Am I Keeping Healthy Personal Boundaries?

Signs of Healthy Boundaries

Healthy personal boundaries encourage me to . . .

- Seek God first.
- Recognize Christ's presence.
- Depend on the Spirit's intercession.
- Consider my well-being and behavior.
- Accept responsibility for my own limits.
- Reject taking responsibility for my grown children.
- Choose when and how to say yes or no.
- Identify, understand, and influence my emotions.
- Confront guilt, shame, and self-accusation.
- Nurture a safe place within my heart where love thrives.
- Recognize and support my grown children's boundaries as well as my own.

Types of Mutually Beneficial Boundaries

My personal boundaries are created externally through the choices I make about my use of time and geographical nearness or distance, and internally by the physical, emotional, spiritual, and mental limits I establish as I think and act responsibly *toward* others and *for* myself.[2] Second-stage parenting boundaries are mutually beneficial for my grown children and me as I clearly and consistently:

- Live my life with a well-defined picture of what I will and won't do for them.
- Set limits in a considerate, firm, and non-patronizing manner.
- Learn when to say no (or yes) to them without an apology, explanation, or excuse.

- Arrange visits when it's a good fit for their schedule and mine.
- Adjust my expectations to recognize, support, and promote their independence.
- Choose how I will allow myself to be treated by them.
- Refuse to condone, make excuses for, or cover up their unwise or unhealthy behavior.
- Respect my own as well as their privacy.
- Preserve my integrity by living authentically instead of using people-pleasing behavior to gain their love and approval.
- Determine limits concerning how much, when, and for what things I will provide my material support.
- Provide clear ground rules in advance.
- Value my time and personal space as well as theirs.
- Leave the parenting role up to them when it comes to my grandchildren (unless I'm asked to accept this responsibility when a special need arises).
- Request they contact me prior to coming over.
- Permit them to clean up their own messes.
- Attend to my needs and emotions.
- Recognize that their needs and emotions are not more or less important than my own.
- Stop feeling responsible for the choices they make.
- Determine and follow through on consequences for unacceptable behavior.

Questions About Boundaries

1. What are the benefits and costs associated with the boundaries I keep?

2. What aspects of my internal and external boundaries can I change and control?

3. In what areas do my boundaries most need my attention?

4. What changes am I willing make to establish new boundaries or reinforce old boundaries?

5. When my grown child resists my boundaries, how will I respond in love?

6. Whom will I ask for additional boundary support?

7. What additional resources (such as books, church-based classes, online sites, podcasts, and local support groups) are available to me as I learn more about setting healthy boundaries for myself?

8. What are some examples of boundaries I've set with my grown child that resulted in beneficial outcomes?

9. When I think about areas where I carry too much responsibility for my grown child's life, is there anything that comes to mind?

Starting the Conversation

Is it time to talk with your grown child about setting boundaries? If so, you can intentionally begin the conversation by sitting down together over a meal or a cup of coffee and saying something like this:

"I've been thinking about the ways that I've been taking on responsibility for you by _____ (describe what you do that your grown child needs to be doing). I want to make a change, now that I see how my actions have limited your independence. Because I'd like to better support you in taking responsibility for your own life, from now on I plan to more clearly recognize and respect your adulthood by _____ (describe what you will do or not do any longer). What are your ideas about taking responsibility for yourself in this area? Is there anything else you see that you need to take more responsibility for?"

Taking notes during your discussion will emphasize your adult child's commitment to making changes. Write down "I will take responsibility for these areas" at the top of the page, and then list whatever your grown child says he or she wants to do differently in the future. Once you have done this, ask your adult child, "Is there anything you think I need to take more or less responsibility for when it comes to your life?" and record his or her responses.

Follow through on your conversation: Identify, set, and maintain your boundries in support of these agreed-upon changes.

CHAPTER SIX

The Blessings of Shared Reflections

*The greatest happiness of life is the
conviction that we are loved—loved for
ourselves, or rather, in spite of ourselves.*
—Victor Hugo

At any given moment, on any given day, we have a choice to make:
Will we aim toward seeing our grown children as they truly are or
focus on our reflections about who we think they should be?

The answer seems so clear on paper. Yet we know by experience
that when it comes to extending the blessing of acceptance to our
adult kids, our perceptions of their choices have a tendency to ob-
scure our vision.

"Long before our first child was born, I had this great hope, a
sense of wonder and awe, in anticipation of the fulfillment of God's
good plans and purposes for Jake's life," my friend Elizabeth remembers. "It was easy for me to picture that all would be well as I imagined who he would turn out to be."

Elizabeth explains how her trust in what she perceived to be God's design for her newborn son's life also included something more. "Little by little, as I took on the responsibility for raising my son, I started to believe that who he was becoming depended primarily on me. A subtle, significant shift occurred in my thinking," she recalls, "and rather than adjusting my focus in the face of day-to-day reality, the imaginary book of snapshots I carried into my pregnancy remained a fixed mental picture of who my son would one day be. My hopes and dreams for Jake were the yardstick by which I measured his progress toward the goals I set for him years earlier.

"Without realizing it, for years I idolized my own desires and plans for Jake. Seeing him as he actually was became increasingly difficult," notes Elizabeth. "Looking back, in relying on my ideas about who my son would be, I distanced myself not only from Jake but also from God."

Elizabeth shares that it wasn't until a crisis developed in her relationship with her son that she was moved toward loving him less conditionally, and trusting God more.

"Jake came home for the holidays his senior year and announced to Carl and me that he was living with his girlfriend," she remembers. "What's more, he told us that he and Rachel had no plans to marry or have children, even though they wanted to spend the rest of their lives together. Then he asked if they could share his bedroom when she visited over Christmas.

"My first reaction was a pretty typical one for me: *What? Why? Of course not! Here's the problem with . . .*" my friend explains. "With another of my self-made snapshots of Jake suddenly gone, I couldn't see straight, nor did I listen very well. Though Carl wasn't as shocked as I was, he was just as concerned.

"Jake left immediately, and after that we rarely saw him over the next few years. During this time Carl and I received some excellent counseling. Part of what I learned was that whenever I project onto Jake my own image of who I think he is or who I want him to be, I'm not really loving Jake—I'm loving the picture I've made of him. When this happens, I've also lost touch with trusting God, and consequently I can't see or value the man Jake already is by sovereign design in his Father's eyes.

"Today, Jake and Rachel are still living together," Elizabeth notes. "We now see this as only part of a much larger picture of our son's life that isn't of our making, and we enjoy having good conversations with our son about his varied observations and experiences. We talk, we share our views, and we care. Our focus more often centers on what we love about Jake and his life, and we welcome him and Rachel warmly into our home. He in turn respects our limits and recognizes our reasons for not offering overnight accommodations. I'm grateful to God for the growth we've all experienced and look forward to the excellent things He has planned for us ahead."

Like Elizabeth, we're given an opportunity to more clearly see and value our adult children for who they are in every interaction we have with them. Whom do we see when we picture our adult children? Where will we place our focus when we're with them? What will we hear as we listen?

For the adult son or daughter who believes or behaves differently than we expected, what difference does it make when we see and listen with honest understanding? For the grown child who, for example, gains too much weight or drops out of college to play in a band or takes on heavy credit-card debt or becomes successful at the expense of marriage and family or encounters an obstacle to faith that brings doubt along with it, where will the glimpses of God's grace be most accurately reflected?

> *Where do I most often miss recognizing in my grown child and myself both the great and not-so-great things apparent to others who know us less intimately? When and why is it difficult for me not to project my own idealized snapshots onto the screen of my son's or daughter's imperfect and unfolding life story?*

No matter what picture of our adult children we happen to be viewing today, at any given moment, on any given day, we have a choice to make: Will we aim toward seeing our grown children as they truly are or focus on our reflections about who we think they should be?

It *Is* Possible

I can relate to my friends' natural bent toward measuring and assessing with limited vision their grown children's gains and losses, can't you? In spite of our best intentions, how often have we reached our own conclusions regarding our adult sons and daughters, holding on to our finite viewpoints because we can't comprehend the intricate wonder of God's eternal design?

It's such a relief that it doesn't have to be this way. *We have options.* Once identified, recurring thoughts that center more on our own viewpoints and concerns than on our grown children need not eclipse our ability to see and hear them more clearly.

The truth is, and perhaps this really can't be said too often, there are no perfect parent-child relationships. We will not—and, in fact, cannot—love our grown children for a lifetime and make zero mistakes. Perfection isn't possible here and now. Part of the reason we hope that it is seems to be supernaturally rooted in our longing for what lies ahead. Perhaps another reason we cling to this idea, however, is because once we admit that perfection is absent this side of heaven, we'll have to open our eyes and face things as they actually, really, truly are—the good, the bad, and the ugly.

Trusting God is the antidote, believing that He isn't finished with our children (or us), enlarges our view as we daily undergo the growth He alone supplies. Trusting Him can be so difficult at times, but it *is* possible. As we aim toward depending on God to produce His desired outcome, remaining in His love and extending the love we receive from Him to one another, we taste the fruit of His making.

When it comes to reflecting back to our children through sharing with them what we see and understand about them, our hope is to offer them the fullest measure we can of the kind of patient love—appropriate, sincere, and intelligent—that can wait on God's work and trust His good plans. As often as you need to, reflect on the Bible's description of what real love looks like:

> Love never gives up.
> Love cares more for others than for self.
> Love doesn't want what it doesn't have.
> Love doesn't strut,
> Doesn't have a swelled head,
> Doesn't force itself on others,
> Isn't always "me first,"
> Doesn't fly off the handle,
> Doesn't keep score of the sins of others,
> Doesn't revel when others grovel,

Takes pleasure in the flowering of truth,
Puts up with anything,
Trusts God always,
Always looks for the best,
Never looks back,
But keeps going to the end. (1 Corinthians 13:4-7, MSG)

Do we treasure our grown children's God-given freedom? If so, our powerlessness, rather than hindering us from accepting, affirming, appreciating, and attending to them as they are, can lead us toward loving them with our eyes wide open.

Safe Relationships

We like to think of a safe relationship as one that does three things:
1. Draws us closer to God.
2. Draws us closer to others.
3. Helps us become the real person God created us to be.

The Bible refers to these three areas of spiritual growth. We fulfill the greatest commandment, to love God [Matthew 22:37-38]. We keep the second commandment, to love each other [Matthew 22:39]. And we grow into that particular person that God created us to be, accomplishing the tasks he designed for us [Ephesians. 2:10]. . . .

A "safe person" is someone who . . .

• accepts me just like I am.
• loves me no matter how I am being or what I do.
• whose influence develops my ability to love and be responsible.
• who gives me an opportunity to grow.
• who increases love within me.

"It's easy for me to become discouraged and feel frustrated when my dreams for my daughter don't line up with what I think should be happening at this point in her life," observes Michelle. "I consequently lose my joy when I'm with Caitlin and find it difficult to center attention on the amazing person she already is. Our interaction really does become more about me and less about her. When this happens, I often recover a more loving focus by asking myself, *Am I trusting God here? Where is He already working in this? How does He want me to respond?*"

Eric agrees that he shares a similar inclination toward tunnel vision when it comes to listening and responding to his grown children.

- I can be myself around.
- who allows me to be on the outside what I am on the inside.
- who helps me deny myself for others and God. . . .
- who allows me to become the me God sees in me.
- whose life touches mine and leaves me better for it.
- who touches my life and draws me closer to who God created me to be.
- who helps me be like Christ.
- who helps me to love others more.

The best example of a safe person is . . . Jesus. In him were found the three qualities of a safe person: dwelling [connecting], grace, and truth. . . . The calling of the Bible is that we need to be the kind of people to each other that Jesus is with us, people who dwell with each other in grace and truth.

—Dr. Henry Cloud and Dr. John Townsend[1]

"If I fix my attention on my own point of view rather than honestly considering where my adult children are coming from, I start caring more about what I'm thinking than what they're saying. What's more, it's when I get distracted from my primary purpose as a dad that my doubts about their future multiply."

> *How do you live out loving your grown child as he or she is? What happens when you love your son or daughter in this way?*

Eric adds, "Regardless of what the situation is, loving my sons and daughters comes at the cost of my self-reliance. It isn't about my timing or my preferences, or about what I believe should or shouldn't be happening. I find I most love my grown children when I'm turning toward the One who first loved me."

The Bible tells us to "learn to love appropriately. You need to use your head and test your feelings so that your love is sincere and intelligent, not sentimental gush" (Philippians 1:9-10, MSG). These words beautifully express our heart's better desires.

Sincere and intelligent love waits as it watches with eyes wide open. Such love isn't afraid of seeing and accepting the truth. It refuses to hide, run, or shrink away from the truth; will not allow us to revamp, embellish, or otherwise glamorize the truth; and helps us know how and when to share the truth with humility, compassion, and grace.

Will we allow our grown children to bring out the best or the worst in us? By loving them honestly, we won't depend on how they see or act toward us to determine how we see and act toward them.

In Grace and Truth

Grace and truth enable us to see and accept others as we want to be seen and accepted ourselves. Consider the following examples. Taken as a starting point, each statement represents an initial impression—a quick personal assessment that could either lead toward greater understanding of one's grown child or become a recurrent focus that hinders the relationship and blocks shared reflections.

If such thoughts (if not identical circumstances) come up for you, how will you avoid limiting your perspective of the situation at hand and expand your view? Using silent questions like the following in response can encourage your love for your daughter or son to grow in grace and truth:

> **STATEMENT:** *My daughter's perfectionism is clearly making life harder for herself and those around her. I feel like it's my fault that this is happening.*
> **POSSIBLE RESPONSE:** When things go well, I don't stay up all night wondering what I did right. Why do I take on the blame when something difficult comes up? Where do I need to surrender responsibility here? How can I be caring and emotionally open with my daughter without trying to fix this?

> **STATEMENT:** *I'm angry that my son's children need new clothes and won't get them now because of his recent electronics purchases.*
> **POSSIBLE RESPONSE:** How does this circumstance fit in with the overall picture I'm seeing? Is there a pattern of neglect I need to be concerned with and say or do something about? If not, in what ways will I extend blessing to my son as he loves and cares for his children to the best of his ability?

STATEMENT: *My daughter's sadness and fatigue these past couple of months don't seem to be getting better. I'm afraid of what may happen next.*

POSSIBLE RESPONSE: What is most troubling to me right now about this situation? Is there a diagnosis that her doctor has missed? Am I willing to set aside my fear and take appropriate action? How can I best support my daughter's health and recovery without causing additional stress?

STATEMENT: *My son's tattoo is so disturbing I don't want to look at him. Now what?*

POSSIBLE RESPONSE: Why is this bothering me so much? What's most important right now? Will I choose to focus on the tattoo or on my son?

STATEMENT: *My daughter is the ultimate "I'll take charge of everything" daughter. I don't have to worry about anything when she's around.*

POSSIBLE RESPONSE: Do I accept and/or expect too much help from my daughter? Is our relationship truly reciprocal? How will I expand my circle to include a wider expression of mutually beneficial friendship, shared interest, and support?

STATEMENT: *After moving recently, my son and his wife decided to stop attending church and have begun studying Buddhism. I don't understand it.*

POSSIBLE RESPONSE: How will I continue to listen well and seek to better understand their current interest? Given that I can only change what I can control—myself and, perhaps most especially, my reaction in this situation—upon whom and what will I place my attention in our relationship? What boundaries will be most helpful and beneficial to observe here?

STATEMENT: *When my daughter walked into the room, I noticed her weight had changed and is now at an unhealthy level. At what point do I say something?*
POSSIBLE RESPONSE: What thoughts and judgments have I made that may be interfering with my ability to love and accept my daughter as she is, plus or minus nothing? What can I change about the way I see and value her? Which discussions have we had on this subject that have been helpful and/or hurtful? How will I attend to my own issues related to eating and body image without projecting them onto her?

STATEMENT: *My son says he wants to settle down, but his ongoing relationships with women definitely aren't leading him in that direction. I wish he wouldn't act like that.*
POSSIBLE RESPONSE: How am I trying to protect my son now that he lives on his own? Is it working? What can I do instead? What do I need to let go of, trust God with, and stop attempting to change when it comes to the current circumstances or lifestyle choices I disagree with, don't like, and can't approve of?

STATEMENT: *My grown kids are absolutely wonderful—the best ever. I wouldn't change anything about them.*
POSSIBLE RESPONSE: Is there anything I'm not willing to honestly look at and see realistically in my grown children's

lives because it doesn't fit my idealized picture of them? What do they think my love for them is based on? What is my love for them based on? How will I choose to broaden my understanding of who my adult children actually are and encourage my love for them to grow?

STATEMENT: *My son was always the troublemaker in the family. Still is.*

POSSIBLE RESPONSE: What happens to the way I see my son when I think or say this? When I place this label on him, how does this viewpoint diminish my ability to know, understand, and love him? What God-given qualities, strengths, and attributes do I see reflected in my grown child that I would like to encourage and bring more attention to from now on?

In the midst of life as it actually is, we may temporarily dismiss or forget God's grand design through which He blesses us with freedom and uniqueness—the combination of feelings, thoughts, desires, ideas, and experiences unlike anyone else. The fact that our Father loves and accepts us even when He can't agree with us is the best example of love we'll ever have.

One of the greatest gifts we can give our children, no matter how old they are, is the blessing of shared reflections—a mirror in which they can see our love for them sincerely reflected and genuinely communicated. The blessing of shared reflections with our grown children allows us to see who they are, encouraging us to go the distance with them. Will we choose to press forward, allowing love to grow deeper, when obstacles to our love for our adult children appear?

One at a Time, Whenever Possible

I have (another) confession to make. It wasn't until my four children were grown that I realized I hadn't spent enough one-on-one time with each of them. Because they were spaced about two years apart, I was especially time challenged from the time the second child was born until the third graduated from high school.

I had read about the importance of giving individual attention to your kids every day, but with everything going on in our household, the moments I spent alone with each of them were squeezed into a jam-packed schedule filled with nearly constant activity—meals to cook, laundry to do, groceries to pick up, phone calls to make, sibling-rivalry disputes to settle, church services to attend, doctor's visits to go to . . . We did it all, and we usually did everything en masse.

Some women seem to thrive in this kind of environment. I did, up to a point. Then I felt exhausted. The time I had left to myself during those years was minuscule compared to the quiet hours I spend alone today.

My childhood had left me poorly equipped to manage such a large household. When it came to parenting, I often felt as if I was learning from scratch. This left me with the sense that if I just tried harder, did more, and kept going when all else failed with my own kids, I could achieve the kind of family I always wanted.

Well, not surprisingly, trying harder and doing more was not the answer, and eventually I couldn't keep going that way any longer. That's when God opened the door to discovering the beauty of His peace.

Ever since, I've continued learning new things about what it means to listen. Although I was often too busy to stop, sit down, and listen well while my children were younger, too preoccupied with my own agenda to pay closer attention to their words, and too tired to more clearly hear them because my thoughts were racing toward the next twenty things that needed to be done, I'm thankful that I have had, and still have, countless opportunities to stop, sit down, listen well, pay closer attention, and more clearly hear them now, one at a time.

Though I can't go back, by God's grace and with His help, I don't let the past zap today of its life-giving moments and one-and-only occasions as they come up with my grown children.

How about you?

The Skill Worth Learning

Our willingness to consider our grown children and listen to them with a patient heart enables us to understand them as they actually are. Even though they're adults now, our listening ability and responses still matter. It's not too late to change, to learn, to grow, and to bless them with our warm and accurate shared reflections.

While hearing is a physiological process, listening is much more complex. It's a learned skill and, therefore, an ability acquired by choice. It's active rather than passive, a psychological as well as a spiritual activity. In other words, listening doesn't just happen. Time, energy, and discipline are required on the part of the person doing the listening.

A proficient listener does more than just sit there and listen. She or he attends to the other person, seeking to understand what is being said, remembering the essence of what has been shared, and responding with thoughtful care and consideration.

The following suggestions may be helpful to keep in mind as

you seek to more effectively empathize with and actively listen to your grown child:[2]

- Arrange for time together alone, away from interruptions.
- Set aside distracting thoughts and competing concerns during the conversation.
- Pray silently for insight and understanding as you listen, asking God for guidance and wisdom.
- Improve your listening ability by removing or reducing, when possible, any barriers to your listening, such as: internal chatter (e.g., worries, activity planning, running thoughts), talking/saying/telling too much, external noise, hearing problems, false assumptions, shame, fear of silence, electronic devices, and media interference (TV, radio, Muzak).
- While listening, watch for your adult child's cues that may help you identify and appreciate his/her thoughts and emotions: How does he appear to be feeling? What is the sound and rhythm of her speech? Is she tense or relaxed?
- Name the emotions you notice silently, as accurately as you are able. The emotions expressed may be subtle or blatant, obvious or hidden. What are you seeing, hearing, and perceiving that confirms what the feelings are?
- Reflect on the feelings you observe. After identifying what you think the feeling is, let your child know what you are hearing. Say something like, "It seems to me you're feeling . . ." or "It sounds like you are . . ."
- Rather than asking questions to satisfy your curiosity, ask questions (if such questions won't be distracting) to help you better understand and value where your son or daughter is coming from, such as:

- "What do you want to say to me that I don't seem to be hearing?"
- "Is there something you're willing to share with me about how I can be a better mom/dad?"
- "Will you let me know when you need more of my (acceptance, affirmation, attention, patience, understanding, etc.)?"
- "Will you help me to understand what your needs are?"
- "What do I do that you would like me to stop doing?"
- "Where do you most want/need my support right now?"
- "Will you let me know when you feel (disappointed, angry, misunderstood, hurt, etc.)?"

• Avoid as much as possible defensive listening behaviors [see the following section].

• Focus your responses on your child instead of on . . . what is being said.

• Recognize and affirm your son or daughter for who he or she is, instead of who you want him or her to be.

• Talk to God when talking with your grown child isn't possible. He will listen to you.

Step Away from Defensive Listening

If you find yourself becoming defensive while you're listening to your adult child, this will interfere with your ability to actively hear and respond to him or her. Improve your listening skills by avoiding these faulty listening behaviors:

• Explaining
• Criticizing
• Competing—talking about your own experiences

- Daydreaming
- Complaining
- Sugarcoating—denying your son's or daughter's feelings by putting an optimistic spin on your responses
- Advising without being asked for your opinion
- Tuning out—assuming you know what your adult child is going to say or that you've heard it before
- Completing your grown child's sentences
- Projecting—assuming you know how it feels to be in your adult child's position
- Judging
- Ambushing
- Distancing—acting as if you already know how your son or daughter feels
- Escaping—allowing yourself to be distracted to escape uncomfortable emotions
- Scapegoating—hiding your faults by laying blame on someone else
- Expressing your feelings of frustration or impatience
- Interrupting

Remembering that listening isn't a natural process (like hearing) can encourage us to keep acquiring the needed skills to put our love into action with our grown children. By recognizing the barriers to listening, learning new skills, and being willing to make the effort required, we *can* improve our ability to listen to and share our reflections with our sons and daughters.

Words to Remember

- Friends love through all kinds of weather, and families stick together in all kinds of trouble. (Proverbs 17:17, MSG)

- Be patient with each person, attentive to individual needs. And be careful that when you get on each other's nerves you don't snap at each other. Look for the best in each other, and always do your best to bring it out. (1 Thessalonians 5:14b-15, MSG)

Real Adults Share Their Stories

Hey, Mom,

I woke up with you on my heart. After spending some time in prayer, I thought you would enjoy hearing me reflect back to you today what I've heard you express to me at different times in my life. . . .

1. I love you for you—not only for what you are to me (a friend and mentor as well as my mother) but simply for who you are.
2. You aren't a means to an end to me—our relationship isn't about what I can get from you or who I want you to be for me.
3. God is at work in and through us—He makes all things new and always wants us to help each other think, grow, learn, change, etc., from knowing one another so well (and for so long!).
4. Ours is a two-way, adult-to-adult relationship—one in which we benefit most by giving, receiving, and sharing who we are together, on both sides.
5. You can count on me—that's what friendship is all about. We weren't created to be alone or to do life all by ourselves.
6. I will fail you or let you down at times because I'm not a perfect person—I'm weak and won't always be or do what you would like me to be and do.

7. I will do my best to love you the best I can, each and every day, for as long as I live—I'm so thankful that you are in my life.

You are an amazing woman, Mom, with a heart of gold. I love you and enjoy our quality sharing and time together very much. You are a blessing to me in so many ways!

Love,
Arianna

For Personal Reflection

1. Knowing that my words and actions are the external reflections of what is going on inside my mind and heart helps me see . . .
2. With God's love as my example, I can grow in my ability to love my grown child with more . . .
3. Recognizing and affirming my grown child for who he or she is, instead of what I want him or her to be, happens best when . . .

Prayers

Praying God's Blessing for My Family
May the Master take us by the hand and lead us along the path of God's love and Christ's endurance. (Adaptation of 2 Thessalonians 3:5, MSG)

Praying God's Blessing for My Grown Child
Now to Him who is able to keep you from stumbling, and to make you stand in the presence of His glory blameless with great joy, to

the only God our Savior, through Jesus Christ our Lord, be glory, majesty, dominion and authority, before all time and now and forever. Amen. (Jude verses 24-25, NASB)

Blessings Now

- Recognize God's unique, never-to-be-repeated, astoundingly amazing creation, regardless of what your adult child currently believes, looks like, or is doing. See who your son or daughter is, notice his or her differences and similarities. Use eye contact and active listening with focused attention when you spend time in person together or talk via an Internet video connection.

- Consider and define in your own words the core characteristics of love. Look at the following list of characteristics. If you were to ask your son or daughter to name the three he or she would like to receive most from you, what would you guess these are? Choose how you will put into action your wise responses as you strengthen your relationship with your adult child in the years ahead.

Acceptance:

Affection:

Affirmation:

Appreciation:

Attention:

Comfort:

Courtesy:

Encouragement:

Forgiveness:

Generosity:

Kindness:

Patience:

Respect:

Security:

Support:

Understanding:

• Describe your understanding of what *acceptance* means. How has your understanding and experience of God's acceptance influenced your life? What did you learn about acceptance from your own parents that has strengthened, or weakened, your ability to understand that love is freely given, not earned? List the things about your daughter or son that are the easiest and the most difficult for you to accept.

Thinking It Through

1. What Do I Think, Say, and Do When You . . . ?

As you read through the following list, consider any situations that apply to your grown child's behavior. How have you responded when your grown child expresses these actions or behaviors? What do you want to think, say, and do differently in the future?

Say, "I'm sorry":

Break a promise:

Get angry:

Talk without listening:

Share your feelings:

Ignore me:

Ask for my opinion:

Interrupt something I'm saying:

Act superior:

Do something embarrassing:

Invite me to dinner:

Wear clothing I dislike:

Complain about me:

Follow my advice:

Use profanity in my presence:

Gain/lose too much weight:

Tune out:

Forgive me:

Ask me for money:

Assume you're right and I'm wrong:

Drop by uninvited:

Borrow or take something without asking:

Forget an important date:

Disrespect my beliefs:

Spend too much money:

Bring me coffee or a meal:

Expect me to take care of you:

Evade taking responsibility for yourself:

Get a tattoo:

Smoke:

Demonstrate impatience:

Talk about your sexuality:

Assume I agree with you when I don't:

Send me a card:

Neglect your health:

Serve your community:

Show sadness:

Forget to return my phone calls or e-mail:

Additional personal examples:

2. What Do You Think, Say, and Do When I . . . ?

Taking into account your grown child's perspective, make your own list of some of the actions and behaviors you engage in that enhance or detract from your relationship. How does he or she respond? What thoughts, words, and actions accompany his or her reaction? Are there any changes you would like to make?

CHAPTER SEVEN

The Blessings of Perseverance and Peacekeeping

The quality of mercy is not strain'd,
It droppeth as the gentle rain from heaven
Upon the place beneath. It is twice blest:
It blesseth him that gives and him that takes.
—WILLIAM SHAKESPEARE,
THE MERCHANT OF VENICE

"Do not lose your inward peace for anything whatsoever, even if your whole world seems upset. Commend all to God, and then lie still and be at rest in His bosom," the seventeenth-century French spiritual director Francis de Sales once observed.

Reading these words after an almost sleepless night, I couldn't help raising my eyebrows. Only hours before, my level of anger about our oldest son's chronic illness had reached the boiling point, threatening to bubble over onto everyone around me.

Forget fitting into my daily spiritual practice the wise words of Francis de Sales about not losing my inward peace for anything whatsoever. I was thinking more along the lines of something else I had recently reread: "Go ahead and be angry. You do well to be angry—but don't use your anger as fuel for revenge. And don't stay angry. Don't go to bed angry. Don't give the Devil that kind of foothold in your life" (Ephesians 4:26-27, MSG).

On this occasion, I was mad enough about my son's latest round of suffering that letting off some steam before the sun went down seemed like a pretty good idea. So, rather than scream, yell, cry, or break a few dishes, I took a deep breath and headed straight for our kitchen's recycling bin.

After gathering up a dozen or more empty jars, I loaded the items into a Sam's Club insulated carrier, zipped the protective cover shut, searched for and found a hammer, walked into the backyard, located a secluded spot where (I thought) no one could see me, laid the padded bag down on a cement path, and started pummeling the stowed glass into a safely packaged pile of slivers and shards.

"So, how's the therapy coming along?" Dave asked me consolingly ten minutes later, just before offering one of his best supportive hugs.

Granted, the previous day I could have retreated to my room,

How do you recognize anger in yourself? What aspects in your relationship with your grown child appear to positively and negatively influence your emotions? Under what conditions are you susceptible to feeling frustrated or angry?

read my Bible, prayed, and waited on God when dealing with my anger, as I had done countless times before. Then again, flattening a bag full of empty spaghetti jars served an excellent purpose: *I could no longer think or pretend that I wasn't angry.*

No Reason to Pretend

If only you hadn't . . .
    If only this wasn't . . .
    If only I didn't . . .

How many times has one of these phrases crossed our minds when our grown children undergo or do something we don't like and can't control?

Our adult kids still can have a powerful influence on our feelings, thoughts, and moods as the enduring bond we share continues to connect our emotions with their life encounters and experiences. Yet how we interpret and respond to what we're feeling is up to us. No one can actually cause us to feel, think, act, or respond in a certain way.

You and I have choices. We really do.

Take anger, for example. Like it or not, anger is an essential part of our survival. It plays a valuable and necessary role in our ability to thrive physically, emotionally, and spiritually in a risk-filled world. Think about it: Anger is one of the first emotions we experience after we emerge from our mother's womb. We express anger in response to the pain of our hunger, the threat of our isolation and abandonment, the danger of our unpredictable surroundings, and the permanent loss of our temperature-controlled, heartbeat-accompanied constant comfort in the womb.

Because our anger is designed to act as a life-giving warning when something important to us is threatened, its immediate power to capture our attention is physiologically unavoidable: racing pulse . . . faster breathing . . . tightened muscles . . . disturbed digestion . . . cooler skin . . . sharpened focus. Our anger is a package deal, mediated by and through our autonomic nervous system, hardwired into our hearts and heads to promote our health and safety. We ignore its warnings at our peril.

Given that God appears to have created us to feel anger when we're confronted with pain, threat, danger, and loss—not to mention injury, opposition, and injustice—learning how to wisely interpret its warnings and respond with an eye toward peacekeeping is a necessary component of our life in Christ. Anger's signals and symptoms, in fact, can prompt us to repeatedly turn toward seeking and finding our Savior's promised rest. Once we figure out how, when, and why to say "No!" "Stop!" "Enough!" "That's it!" "I understand," and "I forgive you," that is.

Anger, after all, doesn't depart by itself, nor does it build up endlessly. Anger morphs. Anger comes, but it doesn't necessarily go. And there's the rub. If we don't deal with it, it won't simply disappear.

"Anger can come packaged in many different shapes and sizes. It hides behind many different masks," caution Christian counselors Gary and Carrie Oliver. "Over our lifetime each one of us has developed our own unique style of dealing with anger. . . . A person who is worried usually looks and acts worried. A person who is depressed usually looks and acts depressed. A person who is overcome by fear usually looks and acts afraid. But a person who is angry may or may not look and act angry. They may appear worried, depressed, afraid or there may not be any external indication of their anger."[1]

When we permit our life story to take on the burden of the resentment, bitterness, and disappointment that our burned-out

What emotional triggers exist in your relationship with your grown child? In what ways do you accept responsibility for facing and working through your anger?

anger leaves behind, it's our avoidance drama in its distressing disguises that builds up, not the feeling of anger. If we don't face and work through the difficult discomfort our anger creates inside us, it will change its direction by turning sideways, taking on new characteristics, and assuming another appearance.

Enter the Silence

Just walk away. This seems so much easier said than done when our emotions rise and tempers start flaring. Even so, the next time our anger is kindled, we can count the cost saved by taking time for cooling down before the fire starts raging in our grown child's (or our own) direction.

"When life is heavy and hard to take, go off by yourself," the book of Lamentations instructs us. "Enter the silence. Bow in prayer. Don't ask questions: Wait for hope to appear" (3:28-29, MSG).

These straightforward directions are worth following when we find ourselves under pressure. Whether we retreat to our backyard, bed, or bathroom doesn't matter. It's here—by getting somewhere alone, taking some deep breaths, and entering the silence; entrusting our hearts to God's care, talking to Him about our anger, and seeking His guidance—that we can best aim our heart toward the One from whom all blessings come.

Change Is Possible

Many people feel that anger is childish, undignified, unchristian, and destructive. Thus it undermines our image of ourself to admit anger. We like to think that we have given up childish ways, that we are mature and secure enough not to be infuriated by all the petty and trifling things that do in fact make us angry. . . .

Maintaining peace at any price inevitably involves lying to others about what is really going on in one's head. This becomes part of a far-reaching emotional isolation from others, but just as inevitably includes isolation from one's own self. We all at least half believe our own lies. . . .

To be angry seems to violate Christian propriety, ruining our witness. Christians, knowing God's loving acceptance of failures, ought to admit every sort of shortcoming freely. But by confusing spirituality with respectability, they can in fact end up denying ever feeling angry to themselves and everyone else. . . .

Anger seems to come from expectations that are not met. To recognize anger, [we] must learn to identify what these frustrated expectations are [and after] honestly admitting the anger, we must seek God's help and the help of people close to us to get rid of it. . . .

Being [made in] the image of God, it is our glory to image his character. It is our glory to be gracious, merciful, slow to anger, loving, and compassionate. Love does not keep track of wrongs done (1 Corinthians 13:5) and therefore store up anger. As we mirror his love, each in our individual ways, we act from our true selves, our way of life in harmony with our very being.

As we take these things seriously in our lives, gradually, change does take place. With God's help, the fool becomes wise.

—Dick Keyes[2]

Checking our internal temperature and exiting a volatile situation will only take a matter of seconds, but the things we say or do in the heat of the moment can touch others deeply. Once uttered and acted upon, our words and deeds can leave an indelible impression.

Writer Henri Nouwen explains:

> Each of us knows anger, and anger is real. We are powerless to simply turn it off and it fills our inner space with added distress. But when, in our efforts to be pious, we eat up the angry feelings and do not make them known, resentment begins. One begins feeling a little angry but does nothing about it. With time, as unattended anger builds in a given relationship or life situation, one becomes progressively more irate. . . . Gradually it is no longer hot anger, but it grows cold and settles itself deep into the innermost heart. And over the long term, resentment becomes a way of being.
>
> Resentment resides in the very depths of our hearts, sitting in our bones and our flesh while we are mostly unaware of its presence. Whereas we might imagine we are faithful and good, we may in fact be very lost in a much deeper way than someone who is overtly acting out.[3]

The truth is that hiding or ignoring our innermost feelings doesn't help us overcome them. Consider my friend Stacey's situation. Stacey wasn't prepared for how she would react when her son Greg got married and moved to the opposite side of the country. It wasn't until after the wedding that the impact of Greg's decisions hit home. An unexpected grief reaction set in, leaving Stacey with a void she hadn't felt before.

About a year went by before Stacey's husband, Greg's stepfather, encouraged her to visit her physician for a checkup. Everything was fine; antidepressants weren't the answer. What ended up helping most was talking and praying privately on several occasions with her pastor's wife, an older woman with five married children, through whom Stacey gained constructive insight and understanding.

When facing life's hurts, healthy expressions of grief and loss help us move on as we become aware of and accept responsibility for our emotions and reactions. We can choose to embrace God's gift of peace so that we, in turn, may share His mercy with others. Though we may be hurting, we can choose not to hurt back.

In the private moments that follow the outpouring of our heart's desires and disappointments before God, we have the privilege of knowing where our best help comes from. Turning toward the Lord for wisdom in blessing our grown children, we develop a deeper understanding of the barriers standing between us and trust in the possibilities of Christ's renewing grace. Like the psalmist, we cry out, "Search me, God, and know my heart; test me and know my anxious thoughts. See if there is any offensive way in me, and lead me in the way everlasting" (Psalm 139:23-24).

Got to Go Through It

Everyone experiences anger. Every family experiences conflict. None of us wants to have to go through it.

The point, it seems, isn't that anger and conflict are avoidable. Clearly, they aren't. The point is that Christ calls us to remain in Him as we keep loving one another, to move toward resolving our conflicts and restoring our relationships, peacefully, with the help and guidance of His Spirit. Our faith leads us to own responsibility for our emotions, choices, and actions, as well as for the outcomes of all our decisions.

No one I know enjoys dealing with a conflict, particularly when it involves loved ones who are deeply cherished. When facing such a conflict, how many of us usually, or always, find that we're suddenly faced with a natural inclination to turn away, flee, hide, shut down, explain, argue, justify, excuse, or defend our position? Like anger, family conflict brings up a range of inner desires that run contrary to developing constructive solutions.

At such times, understanding and working through our own

Alex and Rob

The last thing Alex expected his pastor to say when Alex asked for advice on what to do with his fears about his son's military service was, "You need to deal with your anger toward your son, Alex. It's tearing you up inside."

"*Was* I angry with Rob about that? You bet I was," Alex admits, "though I hadn't looked at it that way before. As it turned out, I had been angry for years, for many other reasons as well."

Looking back at that point, Alex realized that whenever he saw various leaders in the newspaper or heard them speaking on TV, he became hypercritical. His online reading was often focused on topics that fed his frustration with the political process, while his regular diet of the pundits' public commentary filled him with annoyance and dissatisfaction. In conversation, he frequently drifted away from encouraging others, instead voicing his observations and complaints about the deterioration of society. Alex also found it difficult to pray for the church leaders he disagreed with, let alone his enemies. Since he usually addressed these things with humor and a smile, he didn't think he was hurting anyone.

"Without knowing it," Alex says, "my irritation was trickling down to my family through my mood, thoughts, and attitudes. The tense atmosphere in our home reflected my heart's caustic condition. Some talk about seeing the world through rose-colored glasses—well, I was seeing everything through smoke-filled ones. I fumed, casting blame in many different directions."

Not surprisingly, Alex's sons and daughters-in-law began visiting less and less, partly because their own political preferences directly opposed his. He subtly and not so subtly tried to change their minds about every issue he cared about. Arguments were common. The last thing Alex expected to happen after one of their heated discussions was that his oldest son, Rob, would enlist in the Marine Corps and end up fighting in Afghanistan. When that happened, Alex became more uptight than ever, worrying day and night while wondering whether his boy would come home alive.

Then one night he read, "You've kept track of my every toss and turn through the sleepless nights, each tear entered in your ledger, each ache written in your book" (Psalm 56:8, MSG). "Somehow, when I saw this familiar verse on that particular evening, it took my breath away," Alex recalls. "God's presence became especially real to me. I slipped out of the chair by my desk onto the floor, where I knelt with my Bible open to the Psalms, praying for God's peace and comfort as I wept, repeatedly rereading the words '. . . each tear entered in your ledger, each ache written in your book.' "

The next morning, Alex made an appointment to see his pastor. With his pastor's support—and through prayer, additional Bible study, examining the roots of his anger, and reading some books about the

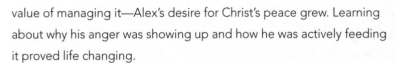

value of managing it—Alex's desire for Christ's peace grew. Learning about why his anger was showing up and how he was actively feeding it proved life changing.

God's grace continues to remind Alex where he needs Him most. Alex says, "I'm profoundly grateful to God for all that He has done and is still doing. Believing Christ accepts me for who I am, as I am—the good, the bad, the positive, the negative, you name it—encourages me to depend on Him to know how to accept and love others. There is more room for His peace in our family now. This gives me the extra motivation I need to deal with my anger as it comes up.

"Since our son returned home from the war, we've been enjoying spending more time together. Instead of focusing on what's wrong with the world and my family, I stick with following the instructions in Philippians 4:4-9. When I give my anger to God and pray about my concerns, I find I have much more space for Him in my life, as well as extra room for joy and appreciation. The energy that I used to invest in constantly tearing things down now gets directed toward building people up. I now see serving God, my family, and others, regardless of who they are, as an astounding privilege.

"Now that my ranting days are over," Alex says, "I don't ever want to return to a way of living that is permeated with 'righteous anger.' There may be a time and place for it, but for me it became a deadly daily pursuit. Frankly, I think I was addicted to being angry and just used God as my excuse. But with His help and the loving support of my family and friends, I pray that I'll keep returning to the peace of Christ, remaining where He calls me to be and acting in accordance with His will, one day at a time.

anger can help us communicate and listen better in order to understand and resolve conflict. How we view conflict with our grown children, as well as how we view our anger with, for, toward, and about them, can move us further apart or bring us closer together, shut down our ability to talk things through or open up our capacity to work things out, put us on an avenue to increased stress and distance in the relationship or set us on the track to forgiveness and reconciliation. Approaching the conflict in anticipation of the good things to come builds in us the hope that the hard things we're dealing with in the present will sooner or later get resolved.

"One of the things I often say to my daughter that helps us work through our differences is, 'It's not your task to live within my comfort zone,'" says Beth. "This makes it clear to Trisha that I respect her adulthood and lets her know that I've dealt with my feelings about the things I don't agree with her on. In this way, I prepare myself to approach the conflict we're facing in a more mutually agreeable way."

"Before addressing a conflict with one of my grown children," Melissa explains, "I pray for God's direction as I think through a list of questions like *What are my real concerns here? Have I entrusted this to God's care and protection? How can I approach this situation in*

What issues are you currently facing with your grown child that you find most difficult to talk about, deal with, or confront? What issues have you previously faced and resolved together? Were these issues settled satisfactorily for you and your son or daughter? If so, how?

a way that will be beneficial for both of us? Where am I at in terms of what I'm feeling right now? Am I prepared to stop being defensive? Have I actually let go of my desire for control about the things I want to change or make my adult child do differently? Am I willing to ask for and/or give my forgiveness where needed? What are the best next steps?

"Often I find that a conflict can be resolved more quickly than I'd imagined, or even avoided altogether, by making this investment on the front end," Melissa acknowledges. "It never ceases to surprise me how often I can make mountains out of molehills, so I like to take a look at my part on the front end before taking next steps. Not everything that seems like a conflict is actually as big a problem as I may initially think it is. But when it turns out that I need to work something out with my son or daughter and I take enough time to ask myself these questions first, it helps me to listen better and speak the truth in love."

Take a look at the following twenty-five common sources of parent–adult child conflict. Some may sound very familiar to you. As you read over the list, I want to encourage you by emphasizing that you're not alone in whatever conflict you may be facing, and that there *is* hope for peace and reconciliation.

Twenty-Five Common Sources of Parent–Adult Child Conflict
- Divergent values, beliefs, and life goals
- Generational differences
- Personality differences
- Sibling rivalry
- Lifestyle habits and practices
- Unrealistic expectations
- Communication problems
- Career choices and challenges

- Time
- Money
- Standard-of-living gaps
- Unfulfilled hopes and dreams
- Real or imagined threats to the relationship
- Mobility and living location
- Gifts
- Vacations
- Length of visits, time together, where to spend the holidays
- Relationship preferences and habits
- Marital matters
- In-laws
- Grown child's parenting: values, goals, skills, and expectations
- Grandparent's role: level of involvement in adult child's family
- Divorce, remarriage, and stepparenting
- Child custody and grandparent visitation/support
- The past

Next Steps

Okay. We acknowledge this truth: Healthy relationships with our grown children aren't anger-free or conflict-free. Things come up. The road through second-stage parenting encounters peaks, valleys, U-turns, storms, and plateaus, not to mention missing road markers, hazardous ruts, steep curves, and scenic vistas. Bumps happen. But effortless travel isn't the goal. Our aspiration is to persevere in promoting family peace along the journey with loving truth and grace.

Really? Do we truly believe this? And if we do, how do we get there?

When our shared history—the sum total of all that our families have experienced and gone through, alone and together—combines with our present hopes, dreams, and expectations, with each generation approaching the future from its own viewpoint, it isn't surprising that we sometimes wonder how we'll reach our desired destination. Nevertheless, resolving conflict with our grown children greatly benefits from all of the ways God helps us in our weaknesses through Christ, including the gift of His grace, the provision of His love, and the persistence of His care in the face of change.

Learning to say we're sorry and extend forgiveness to each other cultivates the connections we share. Extending to our sons and daughters the same respect, kindness, encouragement, and consideration we aim to offer every adult makes peacekeeping possible.

"One of the things that I try not to forget with my grown kids, especially when there's a conflict going on about something, is that it's not all about me. I need to be willing to get out of the way and genuinely consider where they're coming from," shares Ben. "Saying I'm sorry, admitting when I'm wrong, and asking for their forgiveness when I need to, though not necessarily easy, brings healing and grows our relationship.

"If I'm not willing to look at my side of things and consider the major role I can play as a dad in letting my daughters know how much they matter, to really see who they are and express my desire to know and love them to the best of my ability," he says, "I've got some work to do."

Each of us can develop our capacity for seeing beyond our own viewpoints in order to understand where our grown children are coming from. We aren't alone in this, after all. We are not helpless.

In addition to the present comfort and aid God provides us through His Spirit, we have the living benefit and action of His Word, not to mention the support we can receive through well-trained pastoral staff and Christ-centered counselors; resource books, online

Dealing with Conflict

The next time a conflict arises in your relationship with your adult child, work it out together using these tried-and-true guidelines as you persevere in peacekeeping:

- *Confront the issue as soon as possible.* Calm down first. Seek God's wisdom. Untie the primary concern from petty matters.
- *Remember you're on the same team.* Aim for peace and reconciliation as you prayerfully move toward a positive solution.
- *Clear the air.* Has there been a misunderstanding? If so, find out what has been done or said that may have provoked the current conflict. Be ready to make an apology and/or extend your forgiveness.
- *Convey your respect.* Be present. Connect through courteous communication. Avoid condescension. Offer your love, understanding, and affirmation.
- *Explore each other's point of view.* Ask questions. Avoid assumptions. Try seeing yourself more clearly from your grown child's perspective.
- *Recognize and name the problem as you see it.* Is the current problem a smaller part of a larger dispute? What's the real issue? Stay specific, and steer clear of oversimplifying.
- *Pinpoint the desired outcome.* Talk about and determine each other's interests. Positions ("This is where I stand") can be dif-

tools, and support groups; and the companionship of our spouse, extended family, and/or closest friends.

"First keep the peace within yourself, then you can also bring peace to others," observed Thomas à Kempis. Are we willing to keep

ficult to reconcile. Interests ("This is what I want") can provide opportunities for greater understanding and cooperation. For example, if my son is living in my home and not cleaning up his dishes, my interest ("I want to be able to rest and relax when I'm away from work") underlying my position ("Messy behavior is unacceptable") is to feel comfortable.

- *Focus on the current conflict.* Remain centered on addressing the core issue. Avoid getting distracted by any other unresolved or unrelated family matters.
- *Give and receive.* Listen attentively. Share from your heart. Hear the thoughts and feelings behind your adult child's ideas. Help your son or daughter understand where you're coming from as well.
- *Value your relationship.* At all times. Above and beyond whatever is said. No matter what happens. Remember: "Love never gives up . . . Trusts God always, always looks for the best, never looks back, but keeps going to the end" (1 Corinthians 13:4, 7, MSG).
- *Resolve the conflict.* Find the middle ground. Be willing to work out a solution to the problem that recognizes and allows room for both your and your child's needs. Enjoy the fruit of flexibility and understanding.

first things first? To see with God's help what's going on inside our own minds and hearts? To take the long view into consideration rather than reacting with short-term vision?

The way we cope with our anger, deal with conflict, and share Christ's peace directly influences the growth and quality of our family connections. Within the framework of the family, our self-centered focus has the opportunity to be transformed. Given the frequent friction of our needs, wants, outlooks, values, beliefs, preferences, desires, interests, goals, pursuits, and personalities, in which direction will we choose to go?

Words to Remember

- Be angry, and do not sin; ponder in your own hearts on your beds, and be silent. (Psalm 4:4, ESV)
- The beginning of strife is like letting out water, so quit before the quarrel breaks out. (Proverbs 17:14, ESV)
- Good sense makes one slow to anger, and it is his glory to overlook an offense. (Proverbs 19:11, ESV)

Real Adults Share Their Stories

No matter what happens, I know I can count on my mom and dad's love. Even during the times when they disapprove of something I say or do or can't support my choices, they still love me.

I'm in recovery today for using meth. It has been a rough road, with several stays in rehab over the last ten years, and four of those years spent in a correctional facility. During that time my parents didn't give up on me. Their love has been tough but good.

My parents recognize I have a cunning and baffling disease, and they have gotten the support they need to help them understand me. They hold the line and don't cross it. We're all currently working on living with trust and communication, and each day things seem to get better in sobriety with open-mindedness, willingness, and honesty.

This year I started following Christ again. At the church I go to now, the pastor is also a recovering addict, as are many of the people who attend. With the help of the Twelve Steps of Alcoholics Anonymous, I've found a new pathway to freedom. Although this pathway isn't easy, it is a simple program with spiritual principles where I have found structure, support, and a new relationship with Jesus. I realize that I haven't been cured, but I will continue attending AA and living the spiritual principles I am learning to the best of my ability. I hope to continue helping other recovering addicts and alcoholics with my experience, strength, and hope.

There were times when I was incarcerated when I felt alone, and my family members were the only ones who sent letters, called, and visited me. That was very important to me in times of extreme loneliness.

Without my parents' love and support, things would have been much more difficult. The love and compassion they have shown me have helped me extend love and compassion toward others. What we've learned is that any family dealing with addictions and other hard struggles can face and overcome these difficulties through recovery programs, teamwork, and God's help.

—Landon

For Personal Reflection

1. When I'm angry, I notice . . .
2. Taking responsibility for my emotions allows me to . . .

3. At this point in my relationship with my grown child, peacekeeping has become . . .

Prayers

Praying God's Blessing for My Family
May God himself, the God who makes everything holy and whole, make us holy and whole, put us together—spirit, soul, and body—and keep us fit for the coming of our Master, Jesus Christ. The One who called us is completely dependable. If he said it, he'll do it! (Adaptation of 1 Thessalonians 5:23-24, MSG)

Praying God's Blessing for My Grown Child
God bless you and keep you, God smile on you and gift you, God look you full in the face and make you prosper. (Numbers 6:24-26, MSG)

Blessings Now

- Understanding others as they actually are—not who we want them to be—builds mutual trust and respect. When your patience runs out with your adult child, recognize that out-of-bounds criticism ridicules, suggests ways to fail, and tears down your grown child, while in-bounds feedback strengthens and encourages your son or daughter. Establish verbal boundaries for yourself by keeping these points in mind:
    1. Out-of-bounds criticism is always destructive, often angry, and never acceptable. This kind of approach to a concern doesn't work because it provokes a self-defensive reaction instead of invit-

ing a cooperative response. Though statements spoken in anger or out of frustration often aren't intended, consider what your grown child hears when, in the heat of the moment, you say something like: "You never learn, do you?" "Stop doing that, stupid." "If it weren't for you, I'd be happy." "I can't believe you're such a klutz." "What a ridiculous thing to do!"

2. In-bounds feedback is an acceptable and effective way to communicate your boundaries and/or desire for change. It takes into account both your and your adult child's expectations, centers on the facts rather than your assumptions, is given at an appropriate time, and focuses on what your grown child does, not who he or she is.

3. Consider and compare the following statements: "You're late for dinner" versus "You're disrespectful when you show up late." "When you borrowed my shoes without asking I didn't know where they were, so please ask first" versus "You really don't care about my feelings, do you? I can't believe you took my shoes without asking!" "Last year we didn't see each other on Christmas, and I'd like it if you could spend part of the holiday with us this December" versus "You were inconsiderate when you didn't come over last Christmas. Will you try harder this year?" "Clean the shower when you are finished" versus "How about cleaning the shower when you're done instead of leaving it a big mess like you usually do?" Notice how the

out-of-bounds criticism sends a message about someone else instead of providing clear communication about the point of concern. In-bounds feedback helps define the issue rather than define the person.

4. If you grew up with a verbally abusive parent, you're well acquainted with the long-lasting effects of damaging words that send the message, "I don't like you, I don't see you, I don't hear you." Whether you voice off-limits criticism in public or private, it's hurtful to your son or daughter—and to your relationship. Choose to stick with the facts about your grown child's behavior. Avoid making assumptions about his or her character.

   To sum it all up, in-bounds feedback considers the feelings of the other person; reinforces healthy personal boundaries; communicates the facts of your concern; builds up others instead of tearing them down; promotes a healthy self-concept; advocates Christian character and principles; and invites others to consider changing in positive ways.

- The next time your adult child treats you inconsiderately or unfairly, resist your initial urge toward retaliation, self-pity, and/or resentment. Go to God with your anger first. Rather than repress your disquieting thoughts, draw near to God as you think through what has just happened, face your feelings, and talk with Him about the situation.

- Communicate your feelings, expectations, and preferences constructively, taking into account that how you express yourself can help or hinder your adult child's ability to listen to what you say:

1. Think ahead. Ask yourself, "What do I expect in this situation from my grown child?" If you know the answer to this question and understand what the desired change is, you may prefer to express your opinion in a different way.

2. Explain your expectations. Take time to explain clearly what you expect from your adult child. Avoid subtle hints and silent messages. Say what you expect up front.

3. Consider asking. It's easy to assume that your son or daughter knows what you're concerned about. Instead of telling your grown child about the change that you want, try asking first.

- If your grown child won't benefit from your feedback, isn't capable of changing, can't accept what you have to say, and won't gain much from what you want to say, rethink your position or approach. If you still believe your viewpoint is valid and valuable, state clearly the purpose of your feedback and the beneficial outcome you desire.

Things to Remember When Dealing with Conflict

Implement sensible strategies like the following when addressing conflict with your adult child:

- Once a disagreement or concern comes to light, keep moving ahead. Go through it. Pray, take a deep breath, and discuss things as soon as possible.

- Recognize that your adult child may need to be heard first while you listen.

- If you feel angry or upset with your adult child, remember that you're likely to find it difficult (if not impossible) to listen with love and empathy.

- Take time to reduce your stress level before you talk with your grown child. Tell him or her that you'll listen once you've had a chance to calm down.

- During your conversation, use "I" (versus "You") messages, such as "I see your point of view about . . ." "I'll admit it bothers me when . . ." "I understand that you're . . ." "I think what's worrying you most is . . ."

- Avoid blaming and bossing. Approach your grown child with sincere respect.

- Don't issue orders—aim for a two-way conversation. Deliver your message so that it's more likely to be received.

- Steer clear of falling into an advice-giving pattern in the heat of a disagreement.

- Let your son or daughter know you accept the way he or she feels. It doesn't mean you've given in, negated your own feelings, or agree with his or her point of view.

- When needed, ask a mutually acceptable adviser to mediate your conflict.
- Determine whether using one or a combination of the "Four C's" will work for you:
  1. *Compromise*—you both yield, moving forward toward common ground.
  2. *Coexistence*—you agree to disagree.
  3. *Concession*—one of you, though not always the same one, submits to the other.
  4. *Conciliation*—you commit yourselves to working together to make your views compatible.
- Before offering your grown child feedback, stop and think about what you intend to say and why you want to say it. Ask yourself these questions:
  - Is this for my adult child's benefit or mine?
  - Will he or she accept my feedback?
  - Is the change I expect from him or her reasonable?
  - Can he or she make the change I expect?
  - What do I think that either or both of us will gain and/or lose from what I'm saying?

PART III

The Reality: Looking to God in Our Present Circumstances

The LORD is near to all who call upon Him, to all who call upon Him in truth. He will fulfill the desire of those who fear Him; He also will hear their cry and save them.

—PSALM 145:18-19, NKJV

Faith goes up the stairs that love has made and looks out of the windows which hope has opened.

—CHARLES HADDON SPURGEON

CHAPTER EIGHT

Take a Deep Breath

*Don't measure the size of the mountain;
talk to the One who can move it.
Instead of carrying the world on your
shoulders, talk to the One who holds
the universe on his. Hope is a look
away.*

—Max Lucado

"What do you mean, you've filed for divorce?" Cynthia heard her daughter, Laura, shout into the phone. "I don't understand what you're saying, Bruce! Where are you? How can you do this? Who's that talking near you? Have you been having an affair?"

Cut off from her six-year marriage without a penny to her name—all savings and credit drained, the joint checking account she had shared with her soon-to-be-ex-husband already closed—the unexpected phone call left Laura not only emotionally devastated but also financially broke. In the space of less than five minutes, she had been cut off without warning from her life as she had lived and known it.

Holding her stunned, sobbing daughter in her arms, Cynthia's heart hurt beyond description. Silently calling upon God for help, she kept praying as she asked herself the same questions over and over: *Where can I be of most support? How can I best convey to her Your comfort, Lord? What will she do now?*

Most of us have been there before. The news wasn't what we wanted to hear.

In the space of a single moment, suddenly life as we've known it appears to flip completely upside down—capsized by a spouse's infidelity and abandonment, a DUI arrest, an unexpected diagnosis, or some other unimaginable event in the life of our grown child.

There is no heading back to the way things were, no route of return to life *before*. As we look toward the horizon and lift our eyes to God for help, we realize that our grown child, and we ourselves, must cope with what life will be like *after*.

An indescribable pain has penetrated the center of our hearts. Realizing our helplessness to heal the wound, we now have a better understanding of the magnitude of our parental limitations.

C. S. Lewis penned these words about love's risks:

There is no safe investment. To love at all is to be vulnerable. Love anything, and your heart will certainly be wrung and possibly broken. If you want to make sure of keeping it intact, you must give it to no one, not even an animal. Wrap it carefully round with hobbies and little luxuries; avoid all entanglements; lock it up safe in the casket or coffin of your selfishness. But in that casket—safe, dark, motionless, airless—it will change. It will not be broken; it will become unbreakable, impenetrable, irredeemable. The alternative to tragedy, or at least to the risk of tragedy, is

damnation. The only place outside Heaven where you can
be perfectly safe from all the dangers and perturbations of
love is Hell . . ."[1]

To love at all is to be vulnerable.

Reaching out toward God's love for the strength we need in our
weakness, we consider the sufficiency of His grace, especially when
His answers to our prayers seem slow in arriving.

What Can We Do?

I not only don't understand why bad things happen to good people;
I don't want bad things to happen at all.

I can still picture cradling our one-day-old fourth-born child,
Jon, in my arms when the nurse came into my hospital room and
struck his baby-soft heel with the sterile tip of a razor-sharp lancet. I
was an experienced perinatal educator and a veteran birth giver, yet
the sight of our tiny son getting poked for a simple PKU test provoked my tears. This was partly due to the seismic hormone shift in
my body, of course. But I was experiencing something much more
profound in that moment:

Love's vulnerability.

It wasn't just that pinprick that pierced my heart, but the sum

*Which of your grown child's experiences of pain and
loss have you found most difficult to come to terms
with? How has this impacted each of your lives and
your relationship?*

What are your most valuable sources of encouragement in times of crisis?

total of every pain, every loss, every heartache Jon would personally encounter and experience in his life.

If it were my choice, I thought in that moment, *suffering and evil wouldn't exist at all.*

In the midst of suffering, we ask . . .

God, are You with us?

God, are You for us?

God, have You forsaken or forgotten us?

The questions are there as we walk with Him—in the meadows, beside the streams, through the valley of the shadow of death. At the side of the daughter wailing at the news of her husband's desertion, in the car driving the son back to an addiction treatment facility, by the neonatal-intensive-care-unit bed with the daughter as she watches and waits.

The questions are there.

No Matter How Dark or How Deep

"It is the easiest thing in the world for us to obey God when He commands us to do what we like, and to trust Him when the path is all sunshine," Theodore L. Cuyler asserts. "The real victory of faith is to trust God in the dark, and through the dark."[2]

Trusting God in the dark—and through the dark—doesn't make sense from a logical perspective. Darkness provokes distrust, disorientation, and a troubling sense that all is not as it should be.

Think of your journey as a parent. After arriving at a place when you felt as if you were walking in the dark in the midst of an incomprehensible family situation, where have you looked to discover which way to go? Whom and in what have you trusted concerning your grown child's protection and care?

The writer of the epistle to the first Jewish Christians rhetorically asked, "What is faith?" The answer: "It is the confident assurance that something we want is going to happen. It is the certainty that what we hope for is waiting for us, even though we cannot see it up ahead" (Hebrews 11:1, TLB).

How do we walk with Christ into unfamiliar territory, into the hard places where He invites us to rely upon Him alone when we can't see the road ahead? How do we go where the Lord leads us when we can't make clear sense out of our son's or daughter's current suffering and surroundings?

"The answer lies at the foot of the cross. Standing there, we are given the strength. As we gaze at [Jesus'] open arms, as we look to him for help, Christ's courage and fortitude [become] ours," discerns author Stephen Seamands. "We discover that Jesus' open arms are also God's everlasting arms, embracing us and bearing us up. No matter how deep, no dreadful abyss is ever bottomless. Always, always 'underneath are the everlasting arms' [Deuteronomy 33:27]."[3]

Surrender never discounts or denies the reality of our sadness, our anger, or our suffering. When Jesus agonizingly prayed in the Garden of Gethsemane, "Father, if you are willing, take this cup from me; yet not my will, but yours be done" (Luke 22:42), there can be no doubt He understood what was at stake in the coming battle. He knew what the terms of His surrender would be.

But that's not all. By laying down His life before His enemies in obedience to God's will, Jesus demolished the opposition.

Through surrender—laying each trouble before our Father in heaven; kneeling before the throne of His grace; casting all our grief and heartache upon Him; entrusting to Jesus our suffering and sin; receiving the full measure of His mercy, grace, and protection; opening our lives to His love—we taste and see more of God's present reality.

We can't do it on our own. We aren't supposed to even try. Heeding the Lord's call to surrender, we're continually surprised to find, somehow, in a way that is completely beyond our comprehension, "every detail in our lives of love for God is worked into something good" (Romans 8:28, MSG).

Every detail.

Suffering sets us apart, with Him. In our experience of pain, loss, and surrender, none of us are the same. No words can explain the grief we endure, describe the path we travel, or tell what God alone can see and know. Yet no matter how dry the desert becomes, how dark the road ahead appears, or how deep the valley seems to be along the parenting journey, the cross of Christ remains our best reminder:

God is with us.

God is for us.

God will never forsake or forget us.

When Grown Children Hurt: Five Things to Remember

In a crisis, your prayer and practical care make a real difference. Here are some things you can do:

1. *Offer your love, support, and encouragement.* Convey your comfort; supply understanding; confirm that your adult

child's feelings are normal; provide reassurance that tears can promote healing; rely on Christ's grace and compassion. Avoid blame without judging, criticizing, comparing, trying to predict an outcome, or taking over. Recognize and affirm your grown child's strengths, adult to adult, without inviting dependence. Remember: You can't change the situation, but you can be loving, supportive, and encouraging.

2. *Be there.* Show that you care with your time, attention, and availability. Listen to your son or daughter; express affection verbally and physically; talk about what's going on; sit and wait together; limit distractions. Reflect back your grown child's feelings with honesty and sensitivity. Take your fears, grief, anger, and questions to God privately to find renewed strength and regained composure. Remain on standby as required.

3. *Determine the need.* Weigh your options. Focus your energy and resources where they count most. Acknowledge the

Doug and Lily

Sitting alone in the car outside the hospital, unable to drive, Doug shut his eyes tight and let his hands drop away from the steering wheel into his lap.

Lily's kidneys had failed, and it wasn't yet clear whether she would need to be on permanent dialysis. While spending the afternoon sitting by his thirty-one-year-old daughter as she lay sleeping in the hospital bed, Doug had placed his heartache on hold. But as he exited the building, he could feel it coming on—the waves of emotion rolling toward and over his mind and chest, making him feel disoriented, angry, worn out, closed up.

Pounded.

He sat for a while in his car, feeling reluctant to head toward home. Away from where Lily was waiting for the hard answers.

At first, there were no words and no prayers.

Twenty minutes passed . . . forty-five . . . sixty . . . ninety.

Help, Lord.

The stillness inside the station wagon's tightly closed windows made a sanctuary. Doug drew closer, pressing in, no longer holding back his tears.

Help me pray, Lord. Hear me.

Doug's hands opened in his lap.

What if I had done a better job as a dad—would Lily be here today? What if I hadn't been so busy at work when she was younger— would she still have developed the eating disorder in high school? What if I had intervened more often when she didn't monitor her blood sugar closely enough—would this diabetes-related crisis have been averted?

After Doug had finished asking God every question he could think of, he took a deep breath, opened his eyes, and saw a leafless tree standing next to the car. It was covered in sparrows singing and dancing as they feasted on hundreds of ripe berries.

Watching the sun setting in front of the hospital, he remembered the Bible verses he had memorized months earlier, as his questions faded into the background:

"Are not two sparrows sold for a penny? Yet not one of them will

fall to the ground apart from the will of your Father. And even the very hairs of your head are all numbered. So don't be afraid; you are worth more than many sparrows" (Matthew 10:29-31).

Doug started praying.

"Father, thank You. Thank You."

Not a single sparrow . . . Not a single sparrow. Not my sweet Lily.

Doug began sobbing as his intercession continued.

"You're in charge, Lord. You know what Lily needs. Where anyone or anything is working against Your plans and purposes for her life, I ask that You make that impossible to happen. Protect her from all harm and evil. May Your kingdom come and Your will be done here, in this hospital, in Lily's life, as it is in heaven.

"Bless my daughter that she may become the woman You've created her to be. Bless her in body, mind, and spirit. Heal Lily's diseases, Lord. Restore her kidney function. Bring her Your life and peace, salvation, and strength.

"Lord, I need Your wisdom. Show me the next steps to take. Forgive me for where I've fallen short; increase my faith and relieve my fears as You direct my heart to do Your will.

"I entrust all of these things into Your care. In Jesus's name. Amen."

Still praying, Doug pressed the ignition, put his car in reverse, and pulled away from the emergency-room entrance.

Hear my prayer, Lord.

Hear my prayer.

He would return soon, after picking up some things from Lily's apartment, and spend the night praying and resting on the recliner next to his daughter.

hardship, accept the situation, and ask yourself, "What's most needed right now? What can I let go of to be able to respond wisely?" Hold on to hope without denying reality. When you feel fatigued, grow discouraged, and/or think you can't possibly handle the situation you're facing, let God know and ask Him for what you need.

4. *Get informed.* Educate yourself. Gather as much information as you can about what happened, what's going on now, and what the current outlook is while also respecting your grown child's privacy. Uphold your son's or daughter's responsible decision making. Stay in the loop: Ask for permission to obtain updates from medical personnel and others; offer to seek out additional advice and facts from accurate sources; pray for God's wisdom and guidance as you go.

5. *Let others know.* Include friends, family, and members of your support group whom you know and trust by filling in each person to the extent you think is appropriate and most helpful. They care about you and your family and want to help. Talk to them about what's going on, provide updates, and share your thoughts and fears. Discussing your situation with others and praying together about what you're going through, especially with those who have been through a similar crisis, builds hope and reduces fear.

Words to Remember

- The LORD is my light and my salvation; whom shall I fear? The LORD is the stronghold of my life; of whom shall I be afraid? (Psalm 27:1, ESV)

- Behold, God is my salvation; I will trust, and will not be afraid; for the LORD GOD is my strength and my song, and he has become my salvation. (Isaiah 12:2, ESV)
- The LORD is near to the brokenhearted and saves those who are crushed in spirit. Many are the afflictions of the righteous, but the LORD delivers him out of them all. (Psalm 34:18-19, NASB)

Real Adults Share Their Stories

At the times in my life when I've needed my mom and dad most, I can't say they've known how to respond. I know they love me. That's not the issue. They just have difficulty setting aside their own thoughts, needs, and plans. And so, in answer to your survey question "What kinds of things have your parents done when you've been in a crisis that made a positive difference for you?" I'll share the things that I *wish* my parents would do:

- *Listen more, talk less*—don't make it about you.
- *Make yourself available*—please be there for me.
- *Pay attention*—see, hear, and respond to who I am, as well as what I do and say.
- *Offer money, meals, and transportation*—remember how much these gifts have helped you when you were hurting?
- *Leave the past in the past*—today's load is challenging enough.
- *Keep your sense of humor, and smile sometimes*—my world brightens when your comfort and joy are here.
- *Pray rather than preach*—I like it when you talk to God about me, not vice versa.
- *Wait with me*—it's okay to simply sit by my side, especially when there aren't answers.

- *Stay hopeful*—bring some extra courage to the table when I'm hurting, and deal with your fears, anxieties, and complaints somewhere else.
- *Fit in with my friends and family*—it's not about who does what or how you do it; it's about deciding what's needed now and getting it done.
- *Take care of yourself*—I can't do it for you.
- *Keep first things first*—love God, love each other, love me.

Peace be with you, Callie

For Personal Reflection

1. Right now I need greater faith and hope to trust God with my grown child's . . .
2. At the foot of the cross, I find . . .
3. Today, relying on God's strength in my weakness in relation to what my son or daughter is going through means . . .

Prayers

Praying God's Blessing for My Family

Teach us to number our days aright, that we may gain a heart of wisdom. Relent, O Lord! How long will it be? Have compassion on your servants. Satisfy us in the morning with your unfailing love, that we may sing for joy and be glad all our days. Make us glad for as many days as you have afflicted us, for as many years as we have seen trouble. May your deeds be shown to your servants, your splendor to their children. May the favor of the Lord our God rest upon us; establish the work of our hands for us—yes, establish the work of our hands. (Psalm 90:12-17)

Praying God's Blessing for My Grown Child

May the LORD answer you when you are in distress; may the name of the God of Jacob protect you. May he send you help from the sanctuary and grant you support from Zion. May he remember all your sacrifices and accept your burnt offerings. May he give you the desire of your heart and make all your plans succeed. We will shout for joy when you are victorious and will lift up our banners in the name of our God. (Psalm 20:1-5)

Blessings Now

- Sit still, even for five minutes, in solitude. Tell God exactly how you feel and what is on your heart. When possible, sit for a longer period of time. Rest quietly in God, remembering that "he who dwells in the shelter of the Most High will rest in the shadow of the Almighty. I will say of the LORD, 'He is my refuge and my fortress, my God, in whom I trust'" (Psalm 91:1-2).

- Write down your thoughts and feelings. Taking as few or as many pages as you like, tell God everything—He can take it. Ask Him anything. Don't hold back. What do you most want Him to know about what your grown child, your family, and you are going through right now?

- Learn from parents and professionals who have faced similar heartaches. There is a wealth of wisdom to be gained through reading, listening, sharing, and spending time attending a confidential support group alongside those who can understand and empathize. Pass along the knowledge and practical help you receive.

- Understand what your grown child most needs now, including
  - Love
  - Affection
  - Acceptance
  - Nurturing touch
  - Sleep
  - Rest
  - Healthy food
  - A sense of security
  - A sense of belonging
  - Support (emotional, spiritual, social, practical) from family and friends
  - Help with household tasks and expenses
  - Your caring presence
- Use these valuable strategies in the days ahead, remembering what many parents say benefits them most when they are facing a crisis:[4]
  - Trust God.
  - Place your grown child in His hands.
  - Read the Psalms.
  - Consider the cross.
  - Give your concerns to Jesus.
  - Do what you can.
  - Don't compare.
  - Consider and rely on what the Scriptures say.
  - Put God's armor on every morning.
  - Depend upon Christ's strength.
  - Express emotion honestly and healthfully.
  - Get the support you need.
  - Receive support from others.
  - Always keep praying.

Getting the Help You Need

Use any of the following strategies that may best apply to your situation, adapting them and writing them down as needed. Go through them now, and if they're needed, you may remember to refer to them again later.

During the Crisis

Stay calm. Present your requests to God, drawing near to Him in prayer. He is with you and your grown child and will strengthen you as you face your fears and feelings of disappointment, anger, and loss. He truly is the "God of all comfort" (2 Corinthians 1:3).

Accept your feelings. Don't be ashamed of the way you feel about what's happening in your grown child's life. God created you; He knows everything about you (Psalm 139). Be honest with your feelings and allow Him to help you understand them.

Obtain accurate information. Ask questions about what's happening so you can better understand the situation, what can be done, and what the true outlook is for your grown child, as well as how you may best offer and obtain specific help and support.

Pray for those caring for your grown child and accompanying him or her through this crisis. Pray that God will guide their thoughts and actions. Ask Him to help them make the best possible decisions.

Remind yourself and others to eat regularly, drink enough water, and get some sleep. Take turns taking breaks. Supporting physical health promotes emotional and spiritual health. In a time of crisis, basic self-care helps protect one's immune system, lightens the stress load, and restores energy and perspective.

Following a Crisis

Don't isolate yourself. You aren't alone. Other parents have experienced similar situations; many are willing to offer support, information, and wisdom. If needed, ask for a referral from your church or health-care provider.

Keep your options open. Avoid making irreversible decisions. The more critical the situation, the greater the psychological, physical, and spiritual stress; so try to get all the facts before making complex choices. Ask your pastor and/or church leaders to pray with you for direction.

Realize that any loss brings grief. Grieving is a process with no specific timetable. Remember this when you're faced with any of these unpredictable emotions and reactions: sorrow, disbelief, shock, loneliness, anger, sadness, frustration, fantasy, restlessness, upset in interpersonal communication, disrupted sleep, disorganization, irritability, and physical manifestations of stress. Read Psalms 77:1-15 and 86:1-7 to see a picture of grief's reality combined with deep reliance upon God. Grieve as necessary and seek support if you're concerned about how you're coping.

Talk to others. Find people you can trust, and share with them your thoughts and fears. Just letting someone else in on what you're going through can ease the pain.

Try to get adequate rest and nourishment. Honor your body's requirements for sleep and balanced meals. Promote your well-being by avoiding the substances that aggravate stress, such as sugar, alcohol, and caffeine.

Allow time to heal your hurt. Whenever a loss is experienced, whether the loss of hopes or the loss of a life, emotional pain results. With God's help, through time and the help of His Spirit and caring people, you can experience progressive healing in this area.

Exercise for stress relief, as well as for boosting your health. Taking some time to walk, run, ride your bike, work out at the gym, swim, or do some stretching will provide you with many benefits, including stress reduction. Stress levels are highest during a crisis, but cardiovascular activities are known to relieve stress.

Realize that blaming yourself or others won't change or help the situation. Don't waste your precious energy and thoughts on guilt, regardless of what happened.

Request some pastoral support and professional care when you need it. Don't hesitate to ask for help. Obtain assistance from those whose beliefs are compatible with yours, and make an effort to follow their recommendations.

Keep a journal. Expressing your thoughts and feelings in a journal may help you sort through what you're encountering firsthand, as well as facilitate healing, relieve some of the burden you're carrying, and make it easier to share the load later with others. Write down whatever comes up, for your eyes only.

Move forward in peace with God. You may never know why things happened as they did. Trust that God hears your prayers, knows your hopes and desires, and works on your behalf to redeem the situation. Let Him be your help and support, as He has promised: "Fear not, for I am with you; be not dismayed, for I am your God. I will strengthen you, yes, I will help you, I will uphold you with My righteous right hand" (Isaiah 41:10, NKJV).

CHAPTER NINE

Praying on Every Occasion

*Our first prayer needs simply to tell
God, "Oh God, help me to pray,
because I cannot pray by myself."
Such a prayer helps us to recognize
how prayer expresses our deepest need
before the kingship of God.*

—JAMES HOUSTON

Jenny reached into her purse and found a crumpled piece of paper. "It's from the psalm I was reading last week, a page torn from a used paperback Bible," she explained, just before handing me the highlighted sheet. "I've been carrying it with me as a reminder."

Thinking about her daughter's recent miscarriage, I read:

Hear, O LORD, and answer me,
for I am poor and needy.
Guard my life, for I am devoted to you.

You are my God; save you servant
who trusts in you.
Have mercy on me, O LORD
for I call to you all day long.
Bring joy to your servant,
for to you, O LORD,
I lift up my soul.

You are forgiving and good, O LORD,
abounding in love to all who call to you.
Hear my prayer, O LORD;
listen to my cry for mercy.
In the day of my trouble I will call to you,
for you will answer me. (Psalm 86:1-7)

"Knowing you were all praying after we notified you that Carolyn had lost her baby brought us support," Jenny said. "Perhaps it was God's grace. All I know is that as I sat with Carolyn afterward, in the midst of grief, we both felt a peace neither of us could create. I thought I knew so much about prayer, but this was . . ." Her words trailed off.

She didn't need to say anything more. I knew there weren't words that could explain the help Jenny and her daughter received that day.

Our conversations with God about our grown children can lead us into a greater appreciation of Jesus's lordship over all of life's experiences, no matter how difficult, amazing, long lasting, splendid, painful, or confusing our circumstances may be.

Looking up, asking God for help—that prayer of supplication itself humbles us. Here, our thoughts and feelings find a reliable shelter in any season under the covering of Christ's unfailing love and protective care.

The choice is ours: We can rely on our own wisdom and strength, or we can actively, consciously, willingly choose to trust the Lord to love us, lead us, and sustain us every step of the way during this second-stage phase of our parenting travels.

With His help, we can keep learning how to pray.

Think for a moment about the recurring themes you've noticed in this book and how often prayer has been emphasized as our most valuable behind-the-scenes parenting action in relation to blessing our grown children, especially when we don't have any ability whatsoever to control a particular problem or situation. We know this. Yet it's not necessarily our first response.

At those moments when we're confronted by something we want to change and can't control, what do we most often immediately do? We still, at least sometimes (if not most of the time), try to find a way to advise, tell, show, recommend, teach, fix, rescue, demonstrate, or steer our grown children in our chosen direction, either toward or away from whatever we're concerned about.

Usually it doesn't work.

And if it does work, we may have just robbed our grown children of something precious—the adult responsibility that's vitally connected to making the decisions and living out the consequences that directly impact their lives.

Humbling, isn't it?

Like No Other Activity

"I considered myself pretty competent when it came to praying for our family. Then my children grew up," my friend Marianne shared, breaking into a big smile.

Describing what she'd been discovering about prayer, she told me, "When it seemed like not much was happening in response to my prayers, I started searching for a better approach. I ordered books online, listened to podcasts, attended prayer conferences and meetings, and delved into a multitude of methods. Perhaps most important, I spent a lot more time with Jesus and enjoyed praying more as a result.

"As the months and years went by, the Spirit opened up whole new realms of opportunity in prayer—mainly, the opportunity of waiting on Him!" said Marianne as she laughed quietly. "Patience in prayer hadn't been one of my fortes. This wasn't something anyone else could teach me, either. I hadn't realized how much I needed to grow in hopeful patience in order to pray—to be able to approach the Lord with my hands fully open."

Hands fully open. Waiting. Listening. Hoping.

Waking up at 4:00 AM, asking, "Lord, how do You want me to pray? Will You help me?"

Believing we're not alone, whatever we go through.

Expecting the Spirit will guide us as we pray, on every occasion.

Accepting that our questions don't determine God's answers.

Although our prayers may not always make sense to us, we can rejoice in the hope that God hears us and is with us. Trusting that we don't need to convince Christ to spend time with us is where our best prayer begins.

"Prayer is not conquering God's reluctance, but taking hold of God's willingness," Phillips Brooks observes.[1] Believing this truth opens up our prayer lives with God in remarkable and unforeseen ways.

Most important, we need the Spirit's help. Our part is to be attentive, watchful, ready, and obedient to turn our thoughts toward the thoughts of God.

Are we willing to be patient?

When my youngest daughter was five years old, I remember asking her, "Do you know what *patience* means, Katy?" Her answer stopped me in my tracks, capturing my attention.

"Mom, don't you know what *patience* means?" the curly-haired kindergartner said with a sigh. "It means BE QUIET AND WAIT."

Katy was right, of course. Patience *does* mean "be quiet and wait." We read in the book of Isaiah, "Come back, keep peace, and you will be safe; in stillness and in staying quiet, there lies your strength" (30:15, NEB). These are radical, life-giving words—a promise for help and divine intervention in the midst of our family's ever-changing, unpredictable, day-to-day situations. A call to cease striving and start waiting. An invitation for our hearts to find rest in the shelter of God's peace.

Where we're lacking, God gives us His pledge that He'll unfailingly supply our needs. Prayer is the starting point that opens the door to God and waiting on His work, in His time. As we look to Him and admit, "I can't do this, Lord!" He stretches out His hands and says, "Come to me, all you who are weary and burdened, and I will give you rest. Take my yoke upon you and learn from me, for I am gentle and humble in heart, and you will find rest for your souls. For my yoke is easy and my burden is light" (Matthew 11:28-30).

This is it! Here are words we can rely on, again and again, to lead us to our Father, the only everlasting Source of quiet waiting.

There is Someone who cares, hears, sees our need, and knows our feelings of loneliness, joy, stress, anger, sadness, gratitude, and vexation in relation to our grown children. In His presence, the practice of patient prayer regarding our loved ones becomes a team effort, on every occasion. Because praying from the center of our hearts for our grown children requires no sacred rite of initiation or

> *How has prayer helped you develop patience? Are you hoping for something concerning your grown child that you find difficult to wait for? What may God be prompting you to pray about today?*

advanced knowledge, can't be learned by rote or rigorous study, and needs no one else's opinions or advice for results, we can't fail.

No other activity brings us closer to participating with our Father on behalf of His creation. Nothing else we do on earth gives us so much in return. Charles Haddon Spurgeon once noted, "The finest of God's blessings is to be found in secret prayer."

With Eyes Wide Open

The psalmist prayed, "Open my eyes so I can see what you show me of your miracle-wonders. I'm a stranger in these parts; give me clear directions. My soul is starved and hungry, ravenous!—insatiable for your nourishing commands" (Psalm 119:18-20, MSG).

I can't say that I always like living with my eyes open. Like the psalmist, I want God to show me His miracle-wonders in response to my heart's cry on behalf of my grown children. But I've found that seeing more clearly the panorama of His grace in my family requires an honest awareness of the way things really are.

It's a courageous request: *Open my eyes.*

Sometimes the outlook that God has provided in response to this prayer has been astonishingly better and brighter than I imagined. Sometimes I've been shocked by the things I hadn't seen earlier.

This isn't, after all, a prayer for the fainthearted, I've noticed. It requires change. A change that brings with it discomfort in advance of God's answers. A change that every so often makes me feel like a stranger in relation to my grown child. A change that will end my unseeing denial as it initiates wide-awake prayer. A change that allows me to look forward with greater hope and clarity as I wait patiently to see God's miracle-wonders.

Open my eyes.

Praying on every occasion requires patient attentiveness. In prayer we lift our eyes to God just as we are and wait upon His word to us, with longing and hunger and thirst, seeking the aid our hearts require and realizing the role we have yet to play.

In his letter to the Ephesians, Paul used such terms as *remembering, perseverance,* and *supplication* with regard to prayer; he even directs us to keep on "praying at all times in the Spirit" (Ephesians 6:18, ESV).

In prayer we share with God openly, without editing our side of the conversation. There is no need to delete or repeat. Alterations aren't necessary—He knows what we mean even when the words come out completely different than we planned. The Spirit sets our souls at ease, even when—perhaps especially when—our tears seem incapable of stopping or our hearts are breaking.

"Be strong in the Lord and in his mighty power," declared the apostle Paul. "Put on the full armor of God so that you can take your stand against the devil's schemes" (Ephesians 6:10-11). While it's vital to put on God's armor every morning and to "always keep on praying" (verse 18), we do well to also keep this in mind: The battle belongs to God, who does the fighting in the heavenly realms for us.

Brought to the limit of our coping ability, we discover why surrender and standing firm must take place simultaneously. Through

Anita, Marcie, Gloria, Gabe, and Rueben

"There was a night not too long ago when I wasn't able to sleep because I couldn't stop thinking about the things my adult kids are facing that I've been most concerned about," Anita says. "It all just seemed to hit me at once—Marcie's ache for a husband and children, Gloria's drug use and her career and church struggles, Gabe's job transfer to another state, and Rueben's efforts to meet the financial needs of his family by working two jobs.

"Since she was a little girl, my oldest daughter has very much wanted to get married and have children, but when Marcie recently turned thirty-five, she became more withdrawn and down. She had been hoping to receive an engagement ring from her long-term boyfriend when he took her out to dinner for her birthday, but instead of proposing he told her that he isn't interested in making a commitment. She's beginning to think it's never going to happen.

"Gloria's an amazing artist," Anita notes, smiling. "She recently graduated from art school and is finding it difficult to become established in her profession. As a Christian, she's wondering when and where God will lead her into a community of believers who value and support her work. While Gloria was in school, she had a great connection with her friends there, but she recently started smoking marijuana with them because it's what everyone enjoyed doing in the evenings after class. She told me she sees nothing wrong with this," she adds, a twinge of frustration in her voice.

"Gabe doesn't want to move his family 750 miles away from where our family has always lived. He likes it here in his hometown, and we love having him and his family nearby. His company is relocating, however, and given the promotion and substantial pay raise they've offered him,

Gabe believes that moving is the best thing to do right now. This may be true," Anita concedes, "but the thought of having our son, daughter-in-law, and three of our grandchildren live so far away makes me sad.

"Rueben, our youngest, works nearby at our church and supplements his income with a second job doing landscaping. He, too, like Gabe, is devoted to his family and is a loving husband and dad to his two girls. He's exhausted, though, and with a new baby on the way, he's soon going to be stretched even further.

"These were some of the thoughts pressing in on me when I was lying awake in bed," Anita recalls. "Not wanting to disturb my husband, I got up and went into the guest bedroom with my Bible, a pen, and a pad of paper.

"After turning on a light, I sat down at the desk and copied a few passages from the Psalms. My conversation in prayer with God continued as I shared with Him in writing everything I was concerned about—the details, the questions, my feelings. It felt more like wrestling than praying, to tell you the truth. An hour or two later, I put the pen down. The burden had lifted.

"There's a difference between wishful thinking and the kind of worry-free relief the Spirit gives when God leads in praying something through," Anita observes. "I literally *couldn't* worry because the worry was gone. A shift had occurred in my spirit that wasn't my doing.

"In the morning when I woke up, I felt refreshed and ready to pray," she says. "With the sense of doom and gloom I had been sensing out of the way, there was more room for joy in the hope that God had listened to me and was accomplishing things on behalf of my children and me far beyond what I could possibly do or imagine."

What miracle-wonders do I long to see God accomplish on my grown child's behalf? Is there something I need to understand more clearly as the Spirit helps me pray specifically in this area? Am I willing to ask God to open my eyes?

the private posture of our souls, we seek God and His kingdom with the open eyes of faith. With His help, we surrender our fears and refocus our attention.

When we choose to cling to our concerns about our grown children, we find it impossible to find rest. But when we continue pressing on, cooperating with the Holy Spirit in praying with all our hearts, we find our sight becoming restored and our souls refreshed. Through prayer we find the strength to be quiet as we wait for the answers only God can give. Wherever we are. However we feel. Whatever happens.

He is waiting. His arms are open. What He has done for the greatest saints, He can surely do for you and me.

At the End of Every Day: A Bedtime Prayer for Adults

Perhaps you're familiar with the centuries-old Christian prayer called *examen*—a nightly spiritual practice that can be approached in a variety of ways and thus adapted to fit your needs. You may find this an encouraging means of receiving God's comfort and direction as you reflect on, pray about, and review your day with Him before bed each evening. As you pray, follow these steps:

1. ANTICIPATION—Reflect on God's presence: *Will You help me recall and better understand the ways You offered Your love and help to me today, Lord?*

2. APPRECIATION—Review your day with gratitude: *What gifts, events, and insights from You am I most grateful for today, Lord?*

3. CONSIDERATION—Recognize when, where, why, and how you followed the Spirit's guidance: *In what ways was I most open to receiving Your love and help today, Lord? What were my thoughts and emotions in response? What do You want me to learn from this?*

4. CONFESSION—Realize when, where, why, and how you didn't follow the Spirit's guidance: *In what ways did I miss an opportunity to receive Your love and help today, Lord? What were my thoughts and emotions in response? What do You want me to learn from this?*

5. REST—Receive God's comfort and direction: *How will I let You encourage me now as You lead me into a new day with hope? Will You help me rest in Your love for my family and me as I go to sleep tonight and wake up in the morning?*

Words to Remember

- The world is full of so-called prayer warriors who are prayer-ignorant. They're full of formulas and programs and advice, peddling techniques for getting what you want from God. Don't fall for that nonsense. This is your Father you are deal-ing with, and he knows better than you what you need. With a God like this loving you, you can pray very simply. Like this: Our Father in heaven, reveal who you are. Set the world right; do what's best—as above, so below. Keep us alive with three square meals. Keep us forgiven with you and forgiving others. Keep us safe from ourselves and the Devil. You're in charge! You can do anything you want! You're ablaze in beauty! Yes. Yes. Yes. (Matthew 6:7-13, MSG)

- God's there, listening for all who pray, for all who pray and mean it. (Psalm 145:18, MSG)

Real Adults Share Their Stories

After my sisters and I were grown, my mother prayed for us even more often than when we were younger. I knew that if I let her know about a concern or request, I could count on her to pray.

Mom enjoyed praying more than almost anyone else I've known. She kept notes and wrote things down in her Bible as reminders. Her personal calendar was loaded with the dates and times she wanted to pray about something specific for our family—doctor's appointments, important meetings, our children's sporting events, travel schedules, even vet visits for our pets. You name it, she wanted to pray for and with us, and there wasn't anything too small.

Once my dad retired, the two of them spent at least an hour each morning praying for all of us. It made a difference not only to her children and grandchildren but also for their marriage. In these devotion times, Mom and Dad gradually developed a unity in prayer over the years that inspired me. As a result, my husband and I now rarely miss a day without praying before work in the morning. I call him on his cell phone, and we pray as he drives to the office. We've seen so many answers to these simple yet specific prayers for our family, workplace, church, community, and more in the past few years.

When Mom went to be with the Lord two years ago, I knew there would be many things I would miss about her. Perhaps most of all, I miss being able to call her and ask her to pray.

—Debra

For Personal Reflection

1. The more time I spend alone with God in prayer, the more I learn about . . .
2. I'm most encouraged to pray for my grown child when . . .
3. To avoid being distracted as I quietly reflect on God's Word, I . . .

Prayers

Praying God's Blessing for My Family

To You, O LORD, I lift up my soul. O my God, in You I trust. Do not let me be ashamed; do not let my enemies exult over me. Indeed, none of those who wait for You will be ashamed; those who deal treacherously without cause will be ashamed. Make me know Your ways, O LORD; teach me Your paths. Lead me in Your truth and teach me, for You are the God of my salvation; for You I wait all the day. (Psalm 25:1-5, NASB)

Praying God's Blessing for My Grown Child

Now may the Lord of peace Himself continually grant you peace in every circumstance. The Lord be with you all! (2 Thessalonians 3:16, NASB)

Blessings Now

- Seek God's direction before and as you pray. Before you begin, ask, *Lord, how do You want me to pray?* perhaps adding this silent question to your usual practice of prayer, thanksgiving, and worship. As a valuable aid to prayer, read specific scriptures and take notes for future reference.
- Abandon forgetfulness. Stock a REMEMBER box with specific reminders of God's answered prayers and personalized provision for your grown child—letters, ticket stubs, copied journal pages, cards, photos, e-mail, receipts, Bible verses, notes, dried flowers, lists, rocks—you name it.
- Minimize diversions and disruptions. Pray aloud to keep your mind from wandering, kneel so that you'll remain alert, pray in a group or with someone else, and turn off the phone to avoid interruptions.
- List some situations with your grown child that can cause you to lose patience in prayer. Describe in detail what you normally say, feel, and do in each circumstance. Are there any ideas you have from reading this chapter that you would like to use the next time your patience runs out?

Personal Prayer Journal

Pray for Direction
Lord, how and what do You want me to pray?

Pray for God's Blessings
Lord, grant us Your mercy, protection, provision, and peace . . .

Pray for Your Specific Concerns About Your Grown Child

- Belief
- Family issues
- Relationships
- Fears (fear of failure, commitment, loss, etc.)
- Well-being (spiritual, physical, emotional, and social)
- Self-image
- Past hurts and current pain
- Present addictions/shame
- Educational, vocational, and financial needs
- Service
- _____
- _____
- _____
- _____
- _____

Pray for Specific Areas in Your Grown Child's Life

- New identity in Christ
- Life by the Spirit
- Safety and protection

- Confidence in God's faithfulness
- Wisdom
- Perseverance
- _____
- _____
- _____
- _____
- _____

Pray for a Spiritual Breakthrough in Your Family

- Truth
- Righteousness
- Peace
- Salvation
- God's Word
- Faith
- Prayer
- Encouragement
- _____
- _____
- _____
- _____
- _____

CHAPTER TEN

Our Forever Father

Within Thy circling power I stand;
On every side I find Thy hand;
Awake, asleep, at home, abroad,
I am surrounded still with God.
—ISAAC WATTS, "PSALM 139"

Last night, while catching up with my friends and their grown children via their online social networks, I noticed these updates:

- George's wife had their fifth child—a girl—earlier today.
- Jane, now employed as a cashier, graduated with a degree in linguistics.
- Matthew is living and working as a financier in Manhattan.
- Nancy, a married vegetarian, likes bluegrass music.
- Elisa got her tongue pierced.
- William plays jazz and classical bass professionally when he's not teaching at a nearby college.
- Eric is in a same-sex relationship.
- Angie likes Anne Lamott and *The Screwtape Letters*.
- Brian recently reentered recovery.

- Grace has started writing a book about happiness, hope, and healing.
- Joan went snowboarding in Colorado last weekend.
- Cameron shared six months ago that he has officially become a freelance editor.
- Thomas married his hometown sweetheart in October.
- Samantha worked thirteen hours on a movie set yesterday somewhere in LA.
- Jamie founded a company a few years ago that produces "unique medicinal herbal products that use organic/bio-dynamic grown herbs from my farm."

Seeing the faces of my friends' grown children while reading their profiles was a joy. Some I've known since birth, literally, having assisted their moms during labor decades ago. Many visited our home at various points for birthday parties, church gatherings, meals, after-school get-togethers, and overnights. I could easily recognize in each of their photos the children they were yesterday while remembering their laughter, amazement, and questions.

Time has carried them along paths none of us could have predicted decades ago. Viewing their online pages, looking at their photos, and seeing their parents' images reflected in each child's grown-up face, I couldn't help but think about our heavenly Father's unfolding grace in our lives—the risk of maturity He allows us that leads to repentance and reconciliation, the measure of His love expressed in the freedom He gives us to make adult choices.

Bible scholar and preacher John Stott captured this concept so beautifully:

"God never ceases to be our Father, and we never cease to be his children. But he wants us to become his grown-up children. Dependent and obedient we must always be, yet the obedience we are

When have you received without delay God's mercy, grace, and help as a mom or dad when you've encountered an area of brokenness in your grown child's life? What happened? How did you respond? Is there anything you want to do differently in the future?

to give him must not be slavish, mechanical or grudging, but intelligent, glad and free. . . . God treats his children as adults, and gives us the responsibility to discern and decide for ourselves. In this way our obedience becomes creative. It fosters and does not inhibit our growth."[1] How fantastic this new area of risk, this formidable freedom, appeared to us when we were our children's ages, as we gradually grew to find our way in the world apart from our parents and ventured into open-ended opportunities for love and learning. We were confronted with choices about what to think and do and say and believe, where we wanted to go and how long we would stay there, whom we decided to love and care for and commit our lives to.

How different it can appear to us now, on this side of parenthood.

Staying in Touch

We expect so much from our kids. We want them to be God-pleasing, self-controlled, safe, smart, responsible, respectful, healthy, happy, generous, kindhearted, well groomed, capable, and content with what they have. (Come to think of it, we may even expect more from them than we do of ourselves.)

So when we find ourselves frustrated or tired with love's limits, we can recall what our grown children say they need most from their parents:

- They need us to show our pleasure in them, to accept them as they are now and trust God for who they will one day be, praying not "Father, make my child the person *I* want her to be—_____, _____, and _____"—but rather "Father, bless Your child that she may become all *You've* created her to be."
- They need us to set and keep healthy boundaries in our relationship, recognizing that the benefits of doing so will work both ways.
- They need our care and compassion.
- They need our tender affection and durable understanding.
- They need our prayers.
- They need our love.

"You can do nothing with children unless you win their confidence and love by bringing them into touch with oneself, by breaking through all the hindrances that keep them at a distance," the nineteenth-century youth minister John Bosco believed. "We must accommodate ourselves to their tastes, we must make ourselves like them."[2]

If we aim to bring our grown children in touch with ourselves and break through all the hindrances keeping them at a distance, is it really necessary that we accommodate ourselves to our grown children's tastes and make ourselves like them? Of course it is—in the sense that we're to do our best to see and understand our grown children and extend the grace we've received from God to them, loving and accepting them as we ourselves are loved and accepted by Christ.

This sounds remarkably similar to the approach Jesus used when the Pharisees accused Him of befriending the wrong people. He knew that giving consideration to others and being close to them didn't confer automatic approval of their choices and preferences. Nor did it mean He imitated or condoned their behavior.

Applying this same set of principles to our grown children can be disconcerting, to say the least. When they question our beliefs, ideals, values, or approach to life, we may find ourselves, quite naturally, wanting our adult sons and daughters to agree with us and continue following our example—to believe the way we believe—even though we know this is an unrealistic and even unhealthy expectation for our maturing children. Consequently, opportunities for loving and blessing our grown children may be lost.

Keeping our perspective helps. Knowing that God isn't finished with our sons and daughters, or with us, is a powerful reminder of the extent of His grace.

In each chapter of Blessing Your Grown Children, *I've featured someone else's story. What's your story? I'd love to hear from you about what you've been learning! Visit www.BlessingYourGrownChildren. com to share your story.*

The Time Has Come

We can choose the behaviors, beliefs, actions, and attitudes we live. But we can't choose for our adult children how they will live as we watch them change and grow. Neither can we shield them from the very elements that, by God's creative design, cultivate and produce their spiritual growth.

As we respectfully relinquish our authority with our adult children now that they're grown, will we see, accept, love, and prize them as they are, and in so doing, value their freedom as much as we do our own?

We can live in hopeful expectation of our children's future glory because we can count on this: Our forever Father will not abandon the cultivating work of His hands that He began before our children's, and our, conception.

Ellie and Hannah

"When my daughter Hannah became increasingly lethargic after the birth of her third child," Ellie recalls, "none of us realized what was happening at first. She had bounced back quickly after the births of her first two babies and hadn't ever experienced this level of fatigue before. So this really hit her from completely out of the blue.

"The baby was a little over five weeks old, and Hannah phoned us early one morning, around five o'clock. I picked up the receiver, realizing something was wrong even before hearing her voice.

"'Mom, I feel like I can't do this anymore,' Hannah said. 'I can't sleep. All I can do is cry and stare at the wall here in the bathroom. I'm so ashamed of myself. I want to be a good mom. Please, help me.'

"I was so concerned," Ellie says, "and I told Hannah how deeply I love her and that she wasn't alone. It wasn't the time to ask questions or sort anything out. That could come later. The most important thing was for Hannah to have some immediate assistance beyond what her husband was able to provide, so I asked her if she would like me to come for a visit and provide her with some extra support. She was so grateful.

"The next day, I scheduled some time off and found a discounted flight. I stayed with Hannah and her family for a week, allowing her to

"Once it has germinated, the seed cannot remain comfortable and quiescent in the heart of the earth. It must risk the upward thrust into a new element, a new dimension, where it will be exposed to wind, rain, drought, burning heat, and frigid cold," writes poet Luci Shaw. "It is in this new area of risk that its only opportunity to bear flowers and fruit will be granted."[3]

get some desperately needed sleep. Once I got there, I simply cared, helped out with the children, and listened.

"After coordinating a care calendar with Hannah and Andrew's church, meals and housekeeping help were set up for a month. Hannah called and talked with her midwife, who offered several recommendations, encouraged her to contact a local postpartum support group, and advised her to call the OB in their medical practice for more advice if her symptoms worsened or didn't resolve soon.

"At the end of the week, it was hard for me to leave," Ellie admits, "but Hannah was ready. Though she was still feeling tired and blue at times, when it was time for me to return home, my daughter had a solid network of support and an exceptional self-care plan in place.

"If I hadn't experienced postpartum depression after Hannah was born," she says, "perhaps I wouldn't have had such a clear idea about the things that can be helpful in restoring a sense of self-worth and emotional balance, nor would I have likely felt as at ease as I did while I was with her. My daughter knew that I would be able to understand and wouldn't judge or question her.

"We didn't have to say much. Being together was the best thing of all."

Once it has germinated . . .

Once my child is grown . . .

Though I can't protect my child . . .

Though I can't save my child . . .

Though I can't cure my child . . .

Though I can't control my child . . .

Though I can't mend my child . . .

Though I can't manage my child . . .

Though I can't decide for my child . . .

Though I can't create faith for my child . . .

Though I can't take responsibility for my child . . .

Though I can't remove suffering for my child . . .

Though I can't provide success for my child . . .

Though I can't secure peace for my child . . .

I can listen.

I can pray.

I can affirm.

I can disagree.

I can accept.

I can hope.

I can refuse.

I can appreciate.

I can forgive.

I can let go.

I can love.

I can bless.

So the time has come. Now it's time for us to become wiser parents who are aware of the new risks that the entry into adulthood bring but who trust that our heavenly Father's good plans and purposes for our grown children will not fail.

It's time to believe they really do belong to God, not to us.

Time to step back so our sons and our daughters can step forward with authentic freedom under God's benevolent authority.

Time to embrace our role in encouraging our grown children to accept the responsibilities and privileges that come with adulthood as they make their own choices and live and learn from the consequences.

It's time to recognize and celebrate the passing of the proverbial torch to our adult children, and to bless our loved ones along the way.

It's their time, their turn, their journey now.

Words to Remember

- Surely goodness and love will follow me all the days of my life, and I will dwell in the house of the LORD forever. (Psalm 23:6)
- For everything we know about God's Word is summed up in a single sentence: Love others as you love yourself. That's an act of true freedom. (Galatians 5:16, MSG)

Real Adults Share Their Stories

I'd love to share with you what my parents do that blesses me! Thanks so much for asking.

They love me, and they listen. They discuss their ideas and concerns, as well as their feelings, with me. Our conversations can be pretty interesting. And certainly not always easy or comfortable.

My dad once told me that when he asked his pastor for advice about how to respond to some choices I had made about my life, the pastor asked him, "Do you want to have a relationship with your child, or do you want to be right?"

My parents decided they would be there for me and keep caring.

I'm grateful that my parents haven't withdrawn their love over the years based on my ups and downs. "We're both feet in" is the way they like to describe it.

When Mom and Dad disagree with my decisions and won't support what I'm doing, they tell me. I expect that and respect them for it. Sometimes I've even changed my mind.

I don't worry about or wonder where I'm at with them. I know.

—Deirdre

For Personal Reflection

Looking back through this book, I find myself thinking about . . .

1.

2.

3.

Prayers

Praying God's Blessing for My Family

May God, who puts all things together, makes all things whole, who made a lasting mark through the sacrifice of Jesus, the sacrifice of blood that sealed the eternal covenant, who led Jesus, our Great Shepherd, up and alive from the dead, now put us together, provide us with everything we need to please him, make us into what gives him most pleasure, by means of the sacrifice of Jesus, the Messiah.

All glory to Jesus forever and always! Oh, yes, yes, yes. (Adaptation of Hebrews 13:20-21, MSG)

Praying God's Blessing for My Grown Child

May God our Father himself and our Master Jesus clear the road to you! And may the Master pour on the love so it fills your life and splashes over on everyone around you, just as it does from us to you. May you be infused with strength and purity, filled with confidence in the presence of God our Father when our Master Jesus arrives with all his followers. (Adaptation of 1 Thessalonians 3:11-13, MSG)

Blessings Now

- Remember an instance when your mother, father, or a meaningful parental figure blessed you during a difficult time in your life. Reflect on the impact this had on you and your relationship.
- Look closely. What things do you think your grown child most wants to say to you that remain unsaid? Consider whether there may be something he or she has been trying to tell you that you may not want to hear. If so, how will you move forward in love?
- Turn your yearning for unfailing love and permanent security—the kind only our heavenly Father can give—into a source of blessing not only for you but also for your grown child. Affirm God's guidance over the course of his or her life; open your hands and surrender the concerns, frustrations, and/or irritations to which you cling; commit your heart's desires on behalf of your son or daughter to the Lord; hold on to the hope and peace gained in trusting God.

- Be encouraged! No matter how much time you've invested over the years in building the bond you share with your child, you can improve your relationship in the months and weeks ahead by reviewing this book, applying its end-of-chapter activities, and taking time to reflect on and pray about what you're learning. Maintaining your sense of humor—for the rest of your life—won't hurt either.

Time for Your Stepping into Second-Stage Celebration

According to YourDictionary.com, a *rite of passage* is . . .

1. a ceremony, often religious, marking a significant transition in a person's life, as birth, puberty, marriage, or death;
2. an event, achievement, [etc.,] in a person's life regarded as having great significance.

Throughout history, people the world over have honored life's transitions with prayers, ceremonies, and meaningful community involvement. Think for a moment about all the birthday parties, baptisms, graduations, weddings, and funerals you've participated in over the years—those unforgettable celebrations and solemn occasions when your family and friends have gathered together to share the big moments. If each of us had somehow missed observing these customary remembrances, our memory banks—not to mention our photo collections, scrapbooks, video libraries, and digital download accounts—would be sizably diminished.

Yet something *is* missing. How many of us did anything special to commemorate our entry into the second stage of parenting?

My guess is not enough of us.

Part of the reason for this seems to be that somewhere along the way, we let go of the coming-of-age customs our ancestors practiced, and we still haven't decided what to replace these old traditions with.

Wouldn't it be great if we made this change? Given the incredible significance of our grown children stepping up into their adulthood and away from us, why would we *not* throw ourselves a party?

After thinking and talking about what the transition to the next phase of parenting means to you and your family, consider creating time and space for a Stepping into Second-Stage Celebration.

Depending on your child's age and circumstances, you may want to combine your celebration with a Stepping into Adulthood Celebration for your grown child in a dual ceremony. If your child has been an adult for a while, the ceremony will have more meaning for you as a commemoration of your intention to shift your role and responsibilities.

Planning Sheet

Personalize traditional customs as you mark the passage from your previous role and responsibilities into the next phase of family life:

- Invite the participation of your pastor and mentors.
- Hold your observance in your church or another place where you enjoy drawing near to God's presence.
- Feature an "out with the old, in with the new" symbolic gesture.
- Rededicate your life to the Lord and renew your commitment to loving your family.
- Provide a blessing to your grown child.
- Take part in a period of separation from your previous role, such as an extended vacation away from your adult child(ren).
- Return with a renewed commitment to your new status as a second-stage mom or dad.

Plan How and When You Will Celebrate

- Take into account how much time, energy, and money you want to invest, and choose your locations—gather at your church, visit a meaningful site (your child's birthplace, for example), give a party at your home or a hotel, reserve a room at a restaurant, go on a local dinner cruise or train tour, take a family vacation at a national park or other favorite destination.
- Pick your preferable format—public or private; formal or informal; large or small; a few minutes, hours, or days.

- Think about the guests you want to be there—family, friends, pastor, mentors, small group, neighbors, work colleagues, old and new acquaintances.
- Determine how you'll ask your guests to participate—with prayers, blessings, readings, photos, songs, food, Bible verses, recordings, artwork, and so on.

Look Forward to the Good Things Ahead

- What are some of the things you want to be, do, see, know, understand, explore, accomplish, give . . . and redecorate next?
- Where and when can you start?

101 Ways to Bless Your Grown Children

1. Work together outdoors, planting trees or gardening.
2. Affirm your grown children's strengths, gifts, and abilities.
3. Accept the reality that you no longer play the central role in your adult children's lives—you're now a supporting player.
4. Stop hovering. Step out of the helicopter, place both feet firmly on the ground, and change your focus.
5. Please . . . don't pry or spy on your grown children.
6. Watch a DVD, TV show, or sports game together.
7. Re-evaluate and re-establish your boundaries to include the significant people in your grown children's lives.
8. Discern the difference between serious issues and irritations.
9. Read and discuss a book together.
10. Cultivate one-on-one opportunities for your lifelong connection to thrive and grow.

11. Avoid comparisons.
12. If your son or daughter is moving, ask how you can assist.
13. Send an encouraging letter, e-mail, care package, or greeting card.
14. Join in events that are important to your adult children.
15. Set boundaries in your relationship without guilt.
16. Intervene when required.
17. Establish a positive, supportive environment in your home.
18. Include your grown children in your life—ask for their help when you need it.
19. Rephrase negative, critical statements in positive, constructive ways.
20. Gather your family and friends together for a Stepping into Adulthood Celebration that recognizes, affirms, and commemorates your son's or daughter's transition from childhood into adulthood. Schedule this apart from high-school or college graduation.
21. Give a compliment.
22. When you help your adult children out financially, discuss and set up-front expectations with them.
23. If any of your grown children want to move back home, understand the reason why, re-examine your boundaries, set clear rules and expectations, and be willing to confront any issues that may arise.
24. Share the load. Have family meals where everyone brings a part of the meal to combine with the others.
25. Present a practical gift card for food, clothing, gasoline, or air travel.

26. Discuss and affirm the family changes that will occur with your married children *before* their weddings.
27. Create a family-only website or newsletter.
28. Recognize your adult children's new traditions and ways of doing things.
29. Set aside time for looking at photo albums or home videos.
30. Invite your son or daughter over for breakfast, lunch, or coffee.
31. Be supportive if your son or daughter marries into a different faith.
32. Extend an olive branch. Handle conflict with love and understanding.
33. Play tennis, go fishing or biking, or take a walk at a local park together.
34. Call . . . but not too much.
35. Offer your help when your adult children need it.
36. Take your grown children on a trip, near or far, and go sightseeing.
37. Limit online updates, phone calls, texting, and e-mail correspondence with others when taking time out to be with your son or daughter.
38. When strings are attached to a financial arrangement you make with your son or daughter—such as your both being able to use a car you're buying, a time line for repayment, or what will happen if he or she is unable to repay a loan—be clear about contingencies in advance and follow through.
39. Remain flexible.

40. Pay tribute to your married children and their spouses as the parents of your grandchildren. Make a donation in their name to a children's relief agency of their choosing.

41. Refresh and maintain family rituals and holiday traditions—special stories and celebrations at Christmas, Easter, Thanksgiving, Valentine's Day, the Fourth of July, and on birthdays, as well as other annual events.

42. Memorize, accept, and respect the rules of your adult children's homes.

43. Share a favorite recipe with your grown children.

44. Ask good questions. Take a genuine interest in the answers.

45. When your adult children marry, become familiar with and respect the outlook, beliefs, values, and heritage of their spouses.

46. Review your conversation skills. If you tend to monologue, lose focus, make assumptions, interrupt, daydream, dominate discussions, send indirect messages, "mind read," or steer the conversation, identify one of the habits you want to change and how you can change it. Over the next sixty days, work toward making this change, and then tackle another habit.

47. Visit your adult children's places of worship.

48. Serve your community together through your church, local homeless shelter, or area food bank.

49. Attend an art show or concert with your son or daughter and have dessert or coffee afterward.

50. Chill out at the pool, lake, or beach together.

51. Accept the way your adult children dress, decorate, travel, spend their leisure time, celebrate holidays,

and so on, though it may be quite different from your lifestyle choices.

52. Offer to babysit regularly, at a time when your son or daughter and spouse need you.

53. Keep a family diary or journal.

54. Don't bestow your advice unless you're explicitly asked for it.

55. Show love and respect to your grown children's spouses and in-laws.

56. Don't enable dependent or unhealthy behaviors.

57. Recognize, praise, and support small steps and sound plans.

58. If possible and appropriate, offer to pay for new tires or a car repair.

59. Replace fuzzy thinking with new goals for your relationship with your adult child. Set goals that center on the changes *you* want and can actually make for yourself, not on the changes you want and can't make for your son or daughter.

60. When you realize as a parent that you missed or forgot, ignored or neglected something important in your son's or daughter's life, apologize appropriately and make amends.

61. Take a backseat to how your grown kids raise their children.

62. Avoid judging your adult children's families and in-laws according to your values, beliefs, background, and lifestyle.

63. Provide the focus and means for family reunions.

64. Start a new tradition with your son or daughter— Saturday-morning coffee once a month, for example.

65. Ask how you can pray for your adult children and their families.

66. Trace your family's ancestors and share a copy with your grown children.

67. If any of your adult children express to you that they're soul searching and not sure what they believe, be encouraging.

68. Enjoy a "just me and you" birthday meal or activity.

69. Encourage your married children in their roles as husbands or wives and fathers or mothers. Affirm them in the things you see them do that show their love and respect for their spouses, and applaud them as they parent your grandchildren.

70. When you don't agree, try to understand by asking questions about your grown children's decision-making processes.

71. Express your concern considerately and clearly.

72. Offer both generations—grown children and grandchildren—an emotional sanctuary and stability by choosing to stay quiet when you might prefer to give advice.

73. Deliver an "I was thinking of you today" present.

74. When your married child and spouse are expecting a baby, let them know you're there for each of them.

75. Consult a lawyer about arranging your will, estate plan, power of attorney, and "living will" (medical-treatment preferences and advance directives). Inform your grown children that you've taken responsibility for your legal obligations, providing information as necessary.

76. Put together memory albums for your grown children.

77. Design a wall, room, or other pleasing space for displaying family photos and mementos.

78. Avoid the elusive hope that things will get better between you and your adult children. Move forward in making constructive changes on your part.

79. Go on a drive and revisit one of your old neighborhoods together.

80. Refrain from looking down on your adult children if they act irresponsibly or unwisely.

81. Know and respect your grown children's current food preferences and keep these in mind when planning meals, in or out.

82. Forgive and move on.

83. Volunteer to run errands, do the laundry, cook, take care of the older kids, or help where you can when your grown child or spouse is recovering from an illness or surgery or is giving birth.

84. Keep and use a prayer calendar to pray for your adult children and their families.

85. Give something meaningful to each of your grown children that once belonged to your parent or grandparent.

86. Be willing to say no, live with your discomfort, and pray when blessing your grown children means not supporting their behavior.

87. Stay in touch if your grown children live far away. Phone conversations, text messages, cards, e-mail, letters, and face time via smart phone or computer are great ways to communicate while respecting their need for privacy and independence.

88. Talk about your role and expectations as a second-stage parent.

89. Make time for what's most important, revising your priorities as needed.

90. Understand and support the need for your daughter-in-law to be the co-regent with your son in their home.

91. Have a family photo taken at least once a year.

92. Create an autobiographical record of your life story to share with your adult children and grandchildren, including these and other topics: your origins, early years, life after high school, marriage, family, and faith.

93. Don't hurt yourself in an effort to take care of your grown children.

94. Participate in a round-the-table blessing at Thanksgiving and other family gatherings.

95. Learn about and consider thoughtfully the people, places, and perspectives that your grown children value—whom, what, and why.

96. Help your grandchild prepare a gift on Mother's Day and Father's Day.

97. Rather than assume you know what your son or daughter is thinking and feeling, ask.

98. When your daughter or daughter-in-law is expecting, use a child-development book as you pray for the baby before and after he or she is born.

99. Care for your grandchild(ren) for the night or the weekend so your daughter or daughter-in-law can take long baths without being interrupted, wake up late, rest, read, and more.

100. Find out your adult children's gift preferences before you shop. Respect their requests.

101. Shift your everyday primary focus away from your adult children, if you haven't done so yet.

NOTES

Chapter Two

1. John White, *Parents in Pain: Overcoming the Hurt and Frustration of Problem Children* (Downers Grove, IL: InterVarsity, 1979), 56–58.

Chapter Three

1. Adapted from Debra Evans, *Kindred Hearts: Nurturing the Bond Between Mother and Daughter* (Carol Stream, IL: Tyndale, 1997) and *Blessing Your Husband: Understanding and Affirming Your Man* (Carol Stream, IL: Tyndale, 2003).

Chapter Four

1. Oswald Chambers, *My Utmost for His Highest* (Grand Rapids, MI: Discovery House, 1992), s.v. "March 24: Decreasing for His Purpose."
2. Peter Vogt, "Live with Your Parents After Graduation?" Monster.com, accessed September 6, 2011, http://career-advice.monster.com/job-search/getting-started/live-with-parents-after-graduation/article.aspx.
3. Extrapolated from Christina C. Wei et al., *2007–08 National Postsecondary Student Aid Study (NPSAS:08): Student Financial Aid Estimates for 2007–08* (Washington, DC: US Department of Education, National Center for Education Statistics, 2009), http://nces.ed.gov/pubs2009/2009166.pdf, cited in "Student Loans," FinAid, accessed September 6, 2011, http://www.finaid.org/loans/.

4. Wendy Wang and Rich Morin, *Home for the Holidays . . . and Every Other Day: Recession Brings Many Young Adults Back to the Nest*, Pew Research Center, Social and Demographic Trends Project (November 24, 2009), accessed September 6, 2011, http://pewsocialtrends.org/files/2010/10/home-for-the-holidays.pdf.

5. Tamara Draut, *The Economic State of Young America* (n.p.: Demos, 2008), 1, http://www.demos.org/publication /economic-state-young-america, cited in Christine Dugas, "Generation Y's Steep Financial Hurdles: Huge Debt, No Savings," *USA Today*, April 23, 2011.

Chapter Five

1. Dr. Henry Cloud and Dr. John Townsend, *Boundaries with Kids* (Grand Rapids, MI: Zondervan, 1998), 72.

2. See Dr. Henry Cloud and Dr. John Townsend's must-read book *Boundaries* (Grand Rapids, MI: Zondervan, 1992) for an expanded discussion and more excellent ideas.

Chapter Six

1. Adapted from Dr. Henry Cloud and Dr. John Townsend, *Safe People: How to Find Relationships That Are Good for You and Avoid Those That Aren't* (Grand Rapids: Zondervan, 1995), 144–46.

2. Debra Evans, *Ready or Not, You're a Grandparent* (Colorado Springs, CO: Chariot Victor, 1997), 88–90. Used by permission.

Chapter Seven

1. Gary J. Oliver and Carrie E. Oliver, "Managing Your Anger," in *Caring for People God's Way: Personal and Emotional Issues,*

Addictions, Grief, and Trauma, eds. Tim Clinton, Archibald Hart, and George Ohlschlager (Nashville, TN: Thomas Nelson, 2005), 206.

2. Dick Keyes, *Beyond Identity: Finding Your Self in the Image and Character of God* (Ann Arbor, MI: Servant, 1984), 187–188, 190, 209.

3. Henri J. M. Nouwen, *Home Tonight: Further Reflections on the Parable of the Prodigal Son*, Sue Mosteller, ed. (New York: Doubleday, 2009), 59–60.

Chapter Eight

1. C. S. Lewis, *The Four Loves* (London: Geoffrey Bles, 1960), 138–39.

2. Theodore L. Cuyler, quoted in Josiah H. Gilbert, comp., *Dictionary of Burning Words of Brilliant Writers* (New York: Wilbur B. Ketcham, 587.

3. Stephen Seamands, *Wounds That Heal: Bringing Our Hurts to the Cross* (Downers Grove, IL: InterVarsity Press, 2003), 127.

4. Compiled from Debra Evans, *Kindred Hearts* (Carol Stream, IL: Tyndale, 1997) and *Blessing Your Husband* (Carol Stream, IL: Tyndale, 2003).

Chapter Nine

1. Phillips Brooks quoted in *12,000 Religious Quotations*, Frank S. Mead, ed. (Grand Rapids, MI: Baker, 1989), 337.

Chapter Ten

1. John R. W. Stott, ed., *Obeying Christ in a Changing World* (London: Collins, 1977), 26.

2. John Bosco, quoted in *The Wisdom of the Saints,* Jill Haak Adels, ed. (Oxford: Oxford University Press, 1987), 103.

3. Luci Shaw, *Water My Soul: Cultivating the Interior Life* (Grand Rapids, MI: Zondervan, 1998), 123.

ACKNOWLEDGMENTS

I'd like to express my gratitude to the friends, family, and Tyndale/Focus on the Family publishing team who contributed to, supported, and prayed for this project and helped keep it going along the way. Your ideas and involvement made it possible.

Many thanks, especially, to—

My editorial team—Brandy Bruce, Jennifer Lonas, Marianne Hering, Kathy Davis, and Larry Weeden;

My small group—Betty Blake Churchill, Amadee Flom, Christine Pareja, Sandy Tipton, and Sherry Vance;

My longtime friends and prayer partners—Barb Pett, Lori Marcuson, Barb Woodhead, Merry Nell Drummond (d. 2010), Estela Chapa, Sharon Taylor, and Kay Moore;

My sisters—Kerry Olson and Nancy Shallow;

My mother, father, and stepmother—Nancy Allen Munger, (d. 2009), John C. Munger, and Jane Keckonen Munger;

My beloved grown children and their spouses—Joanna Linden, Katherine Evans, David Andrew Evans, Jon and Ali Evans;

And my dear husband, Dave.

Blessed be the LORD God, the God of Israel, who alone does marvelous things; blessed be his glorious name forever, and may his glory fill all the earth. Amen, Amen. (Psalm 72:18-19, NEB)

ABOUT THE AUTHOR

DEBRA EVANS, a native Michiganian, is best known for her non-fiction books focused on Christian women's issues. Author of more than twenty-two books, Debra has dedicated her life to Christian ministry and public service as a mentor, leader, and volunteer board member with a variety of human-service organizations. In her spare time, Debra enjoys fine tea, reading, and traveling. Debra and her husband of more than forty years, David, live in Austin, Texas, near their four grown children and five grandchildren.

To connect with Debra and to find bonus *Blessing Your Grown Children* material online, visit www.BlessingYourGrownChildren.com.

FOCUS ON THE FAMILY®

Welcome to the Family

Whether you purchased this book, borrowed it, or received it as a gift, thanks for reading it! This is just one of many insightful, biblically based resources that Focus on the Family produces for people in all stages of life.

Focus is a global Christian ministry dedicated to helping families thrive as they celebrate and cultivate God's design for marriage and experience the adventure of parenthood. Our outreach exists to support individuals and families in the joys and challenges they face, and to equip and empower them to be the best they can be.

Through our many media outlets, we offer help and hope, promote moral values and share the life-changing message of Jesus Christ with people around the world.

Focus on the Family MAGAZINES

These faith-building, character-developing publications address the interests, issues, concerns, and challenges faced by every member of your family from preschool through the senior years.

For More INFORMATION

 ONLINE:
Log on to
FocusOnTheFamily.com
In Canada, log on to
FocusOnTheFamily.ca

 PHONE:
Call toll-free:
**800-A-FAMILY
(232-6459)**
In Canada, call toll-free:
800-661-9800

THRIVING FAMILY®	**FOCUS ON THE FAMILY CLUBHOUSE JR.®**	**FOCUS ON THE FAMILY CLUBHOUSE®**	**FOCUS ON THE FAMILY CITIZEN®**	
Marriage & Parenting	Ages 4 to 8	Ages 8 to 12	U.S. news issues	Rev. 3/11

More expert resources
for marriage and parenting . . .

Do you want to be a better parent? Enjoy a stronger marriage? Focus on the Family's collection of inspiring, practical, resources can help your family grow closer and stronger than ever before. Whichever format you might need—video, audio, book or e-book, we have something for you. Visit our online Family Store and discover how we can help your family thrive at **FocusOnTheFamily.com/resources**.